Seeing Through Teachers' Eyes

Professional Ideals
and
Classroom Practices

Karen Hammerness

Foreword by Lee Shulman

TEACHERS
COLLEGE
PRESS

Teachers College, Columbia University
New York and London

Published by Teachers College Press, 1234 Amsterdam Avenue, New York, NY
10027
Copyright © 2006 by Teachers College, Columbia University

Library of Congress Cataloging-in-Publication Data

Hammerness, Karen.
  Seeing through teachers' eyes: professional ideals and classroom practices / by Karen
Hammerness; foreword by Lee Shulman.
    p. cm. — (Series on school reform)
  ISBN-13: 978-0-8077-4683-7 (pbk.)
  ISBN-10: 0-8077-4683-5 (pbk.)
    1. Teachers—United States. 2. Effective teaching—United States. 3. Reflection
(Philosophy) I. Title. II. Series.

LB2832.2H35 2006
371.1—dc22

ISBN 13: 978-0-8077-4683-7 (paper)   ISBN 10: 0-8077-4683-5 (paper)

Printed on acid-free paper
Manufactured in the United States of America
13 12 11 10 09 08 07 06   8 7 6 5 4 3 2 1

the series on school reform

Patricia A. Wasley
University of Washington

Ann Lieberman
Carnegie Foundation for the
Advancement of Teaching
SERIES EDITORS

Joseph P. McDonald
New York University

(Continued)

Contents

Foreword

It was a puzzling experience. I was spending several days actively observing in a public middle school. The classrooms were home to an experimental program where students engaged in active, collaborative activities of discovery and invention as they studied their traditional school subjects. The puzzlement emerged from observing the members of a two-teacher team. Let's call them Ann and Beth.

Ann was a veteran teacher with flawless credentials and an impressive background. She knew her subject matter deeply and pedagogically, was a skilled classroom manager, and related very well to students from all backgrounds. She was smart, articulate, and motivated. But her classroom, while running smoothly and being both engaging and substantive, simply did not exemplify the qualities of a learning community, much less an exciting setting for exploration and discovery. Ann seemed to possess all the attributes that I had argued were needed by accomplished teachers—deep content and pedagogical content knowledge, practical skills of classroom organization and management, and a high level of motivation.

Beth was in her second full year of teaching. Her content knowledge was thorough, but her pedagogical content knowledge and pedagogical skills remained works in progress. Classroom organization was not her long suit. But she seemed uncannily on target as she worked with the students, asking and answering probing questions, scaffolding their often halting attempts at collaboration and interaction, and creating a stimulating classroom environment. Her teaching appeared to be animated by something more than what she knew and was able to do.

Ann and Beth worked with the same students. The complementary curricula they taught seemed to offer equivalent opportunities for the development of learning communities. In all likelihood, tests of academic achievement would show that Ann's students were learning a lot, perhaps even more than they were learning from Beth.

What puzzled me? I couldn't understand what was missing with Ann. Given all her strengths, why wasn't she creating a community of learners? She talked about it, appeared to understand the theory and had all the pedagogical skills and content knowledge to pull it off, and was really motivated. In contrast, Beth seemed to be performing better than she ought to have, given her more limited experience and formal background.

I discussed these observations with several of my Stanford colleagues, particularly Karen Hammerness. We explored the possibility that this "missing construct" might be something that could be described as "teacher vision." Karen had encountered a similar phenomenon in her work with teachers at a local high school. She immediately made the idea of teacher vision her special focus, and has been exploring, defining, and elaborating on it ever since, in her research, her writing, and her general explorations of the quality of teaching and of teacher education. I am confident that, in the future, when we think about the concept of teacher vision, we will think of the work of Karen Hammerness.

What I find particularly exciting about Hammerness's work is that it cuts against the grain of most contemporary discussions of teacher education and teacher development. Nearly everyone now accepts the claim that something called "teacher quality" is the most essential determinant of school or program effectiveness. Both the most conservative and the most radical critics of contemporary teacher education avow that the quality of teachers determines the impact of educational programs. They disagree, however, on what counts as quality and where one might find its indicators. Karen's work offers a perspective on these questions that complements the competing views by asking us to consider the path not taken by most other scholars and policy makers.

We live in an era in which questions about teacher quality command a great deal of attention from teacher educators and legislators, from school administrators and from teachers themselves. This book enriches this discussion in profound and significant ways. Over the past generation, the answers to teacher quality questions have evolved into four categories:

- the depth of teachers' knowledge of the content they teach,
- the pedagogical skill with which they instruct their students and manage their classrooms,
- the social and political values that underlie their pedagogy, and
- the consistency with which their students achieve high scores on achievement tests.

These are rarely seen as mutually exclusive. Indeed, they are increasingly understood as complementary and mutually enhancing. In Hammerness's work we see the possibility of drawing these together into a more capacious and comprehensive view.

All these attributes are certainly desirable. Who would not want a teacher whose pedagogical behavior was skilled, smooth, and effective, whose students consistently tested well, whose values were socially progressive and humane, and who was deeply knowledgeable regarding the subject matter of the curriculum and the complexities of learning and human development? Yet the cases and analyses in this volume invite us to attend to another dimension of teacher quality. They provide vivid examples of teachers' visions of their ideal classroom, of what students should look like as they learn, of the social interactions among teacher and students in class and outside of it, and even their ideal images of the very subjects the teachers are teaching; all of these things combine to guide and animate the work of teaching.

These visions are neither untethered dreams nor are they merely expressions of deep political or moral values. They are reflections and integrations across the disparate dimensions that others argue are the key attributes of effective teachers. Moreover, they appear to be deeply influenced by the quality and character of teacher education and professional development that the teachers undertake. Thus they are malleable characteristics, attributes that can be influenced and shaped by the training teachers receive, the institutions in which they are educated and educate, and the colleagues with whom they work on a daily basis.

My colleagues at the Carnegie Foundation have been studying the education of clergy for the past several years. In this work, the concept of "formation" has been central. Educators of ministers, priests and rabbis often refer to their efforts as not only education, but as formation. They describe not only an educative process that guides both character and cognition and informs both the intellectual quality of those who learn, but also the ways in which they combine their thoughts, skills, and values into a sense of person and purpose. I believe that Karen Hammerness's work is exploring the "formation" of teachers in a parallel manner.

And the formation of teachers is likely to be quite closely connected to their own impact on the formation of their students. Elementary school pupils spend approximately 25 hours each week, 40 weeks each year, with their teachers. Middle and high school students are in school even more hours per week, averaging about 5 hours per week with each of their many teachers and coaches. Thus, schools most likely provide the most consistent, predictable and continuous adult contact and role models for youngsters. I suspect that the impact of those teachers on the *formation* of their students is largely a function of their visions of the possible and the desirable as expressed in their behavior, their language, and their ways of relating to their students.

Finally, in communities of teachers, vision is a socially transmitted attribute. Teachers working closely together influence one another's teaching quality in a variety of ways. I would argue that one of the most communicable of these attributes is the transmission of vision itself. Teachers with powerful visions of the possible and the desirable can imbue their colleagues with such ideals, thereby influencing the kind of school context that makes a real difference for kids.

I am delighted with the work offered in this volume. I urge that all of us who educate teachers and who create the settings in which they work take its message very seriously. In seeing through teachers' eyes, we may develop a greater capacity to enhance their development and, through them, the development of all our children.

—*Lee Shulman*

Preface

A number of years ago, I spent a year working as a mentor in the ninth-grade English class of Julie, a student teacher in a local teacher education program. As I worked with her, many aspects of her teaching and the students' learning were visible to me. During my visits, she frequently lectured, but at other times she involved all her students in a classwide conversation and created small "working groups" in which she directed students to address a question she had raised about literature. At those times, she also encouraged students to begin to raise their own questions and to pursue their inquiry together, rather than turning to her. I could observe what was happening in the classroom and how she and her students interacted. I could hear what she said and how she said it, and what she asked her students to do. In other words, I could tell what Julie was doing. But how could I tell what she wanted?

"My vision," Julie eagerly remarked to me after one class,

> is a group of students learning together *with* the teacher. As the teacher, I am not simply providing lectures to the class or even developing the curriculum on my own. In fact, the class is propelled mostly by the directions and strengths of the students' own interests, though it is also guided in some ways by me because I am at least more knowledgeable about English literature. I'd love for my students to have access to a number of resources that will enable them to explore different subject matters within the chosen topic of our work. But I think that vision is pretty far from what I'm doing now.

Julie was very articulate and passionate about the content of her vision and could explain in detail the kinds of teaching and learning she envisioned in her classroom. In addition, Julie could also describe how far she felt her current practice was from this vision and had identified some steps to take to help her make progress toward her vision. In the course of our work together over the year, I could tell that she felt a sense of commitment to this vision.

But without hearing Julie talk about her vision, I might not even have known that it existed. Yet Julie felt that her vision was very clear in her mind and was critical to understanding her beliefs about teaching and learning, to appreciating what shaped her professional development, and to recognizing the direction toward which she saw her classroom moving.

These conversations with Julie captivated me and prompted a series of questions. Did other teachers have such visions? What might their visions look like and how would they describe them? Julie's description of her vision suggested that it captured what she knew about teaching and believed about learning, and also her eagerness and her sense of anticipation. I began to wonder what relationship vision might have to teachers' feelings—to their passions, commitments, and personal investments? I also wondered what role vision might play in teachers' lives and work. For Julie, vision seemed to inspire her to try new activities in her classroom. However, it was possible that not all teachers used their vision in this way. Perhaps for others vision might play a less prominent, even insignificant, role. Finally, I thought about the relationship between my work as a teacher educator with Julie and her vision. If Julie's vision really played such a strong role in her thinking about her classroom, as a teacher educator I needed to understand her vision more thoroughly in order to see how I could help her to challenge her assumptions as well as to achieve her goals.

This book reflects my efforts over the past 10 years to answer these questions. I strive to see through the eyes of Andrea, who envisions her students learning to engage in sophisticated and rich discussions of challenging literary texts. I try to see through the eyes of Kelly, who imagines her ninth-grade students becoming independent thinkers initiating scientific inquiry. I try to see through the eyes of Carlos, who dreams that the Latino students in his school will someday post just as many letters of college acceptance on the wall as the White students. And I try to see through the eyes of Jake, who concentrates upon developing powerful moments of learning in social studies that he hopes his students will remember for years to come. Looking at the visions of teachers like these makes it possible to see teachers and teaching through a new lens, one that reflects both the knowledge and passion they bring to their craft.

An examination of these teachers' visions reveals the power that vision holds. In Chapter 1, I introduce and define teachers' vision and provide an overview of the role vision plays in teachers' lives. I also discuss two themes—*balancing subjects and students* and *bridging the gap between vision and practice*—that represent key challenges that all teachers face. I introduce the idea that teachers' vision may be an important way of understanding how teachers negotiate these challenges.

Chapters 2, 3, 4, and 5 focus upon the ways in which vision shapes how teachers feel and what they learn about their work, as well as their choices to stay put, switch schools, or leave teaching. Chapter 2 reveals the ways in which an imbalance between subject and students in her vision can lead a teacher to question her ideals, doubt her students' capabilities, and even consider leaving teaching. Chapter 3 addresses the challenges and tensions inherent in maintaining one's ideals in an era of increased accountability and standardized testing. It demonstrates how the differing standards and ideals from a new context that conflict with one's vision can lead to doubts, questions, and concerns. Chapter 4 illustrates the ways in which vision shapes a teacher's professional decisions—how a teacher switches schools not to get a better salary or better teaching conditions, but rather to get closer to his vision. Chapter 5 shows how a sense of community can help sustain a teacher and help him continue to press on toward a vision that is extremely distant.

The concluding chapter provides examples of how teacher educators are taking teachers' visions into account. These examples from Idaho State University, Mills College, San Francisco State University, and Stanford University shed light upon how some teacher educators are designing curriculum, courses, assignments, and orientation experiences that make room for the power of teachers' visions.

Focusing upon one's own vision may be particularly important work for an individual. For many teachers, articulating, sharing, and discussing their vision with their colleagues can be a useful and productive process. This book seeks to help facilitate that process. A focus upon vision can be a critical strategy for policy makers, teacher educators and administrators, and those interested in reform. This book can help those educators understand and build upon vision's role as a force in teachers' professional decisions about where to teach, how to teach, and when and if to leave teaching. In this complex environment of school, with its increasing demand for thoughtful, educated, purposeful teachers who can balance multiple demands, we not only need teachers with vision but we also need to know how to care for them and sustain them.

Acknowledgments

I want to thank the many teachers who participated in this study and acknowledge the amount of time and thought they generously afforded me when I visited their classrooms and interviewed them for this study. Their insightful reflections greatly extended and deepened my understanding of teachers' vision in the early part of this work while at Stanford University as a doctoral student. The four teachers who participated in conversations with me over 9 of the 10 years of the research that is the basis for this book—Andrea, Carlos, Jake, and Kelly—deserve very special acknowledgment. Because I have promised to keep their identities confidential (as well as that of their schools, communities, and students), I cannot thank them using their real names. But their contribution has been critical; I could not have done this work or learned these lessons without them. These four teachers not only graciously invited me into their classrooms but also gave time to me every summer for 9 years in order to talk about their visions, thus enabling me to explore in great depth the interplay between vision and practice, subjects and students, and mobility and context. Without the help of all of these teachers, I could not have accomplished this research.

I also want to acknowledge and thank the teachers who participated in the Fostering a Community of Teachers as Learners project, teachers who first captured my attention when they talked about vision as a way to describe the images of alternative practice that motivated them to pursue reforms in their classrooms. In addition, I wish to thank the Andrew W. Mellon Foundation, which provided a grant that supported some of the early stages of this research.

I have had the unique opportunity to work with some exceptional mentors who contributed invaluable intellectual support for this work. Lee and Judy Shulman and my colleagues on the Fostering a Community of Teachers as Learners project helped shape my early thinking on this subject. Lee assisted in developing the conceptual framing of this work, helped me test numerous arguments for studying vision, and supported my exploration of the relationships between emotion and cognition. Shirley Brice Heath helped me flesh out the dimensions of vision and pressed me to continually refine and question my definitions. Larry Cuban prompted me to carefully examine my methods and the relationship between vision and practice. Nel Noddings urged me to examine both the positive and negative roles that vision might play and offered the particularly fruitful suggestion that I work with a number of more experienced teachers. Ann Lieberman provided an important perspective about the relationship of vision and context, the phenomenological power of vision. Equally important, she served as a strong advocate of the idea of vision and shepherded me attentively through the writing and publishing of this book.

A number of School of Education colleagues—David Donohue, Tom Meyer, Kay Moffett, Sam Intrator, and Nancy Lester—provided valuable early assistance and support. Teacher education colleagues Traci Bliss, Pam LePage, Rachel Lotan, Jeannie Lythcott, and Anna Richert eagerly joined with me in considering these ideas, provided many examples from their own teaching that enacted these ideas, and asked thoughtful questions that pressed me further.

I would like to thank my parents, Sarah and Jay Hammerness, and my brother, Paul, for their early and continual support of my intellectual work and of my emotional life. They pressed me to think beyond the immediate horizon and enabled me to develop my own vision. I also thank my daughters Hannah, Clara, and Sarah for giving me so much joy, for helping me laugh, and for enriching all the moments around work on my book. Finally, I would like to acknowledge and thank my husband, Tom, for his enthusiasm and engagement in my research and his tireless support throughout the writing process. Our bike rides through the hills of northern California will always be paired in my mind with conversations about our work and about vision. His loving encouragement and intellectual support has helped me appreciate the relationship between thought and feeling in ways that both encompass and surpass this study of vision.

Seeing Through Teachers' Eyes

Professional Ideals
and
Classroom Practices

CHAPTER 1

What Is Teachers' Vision?

I've seen in my head what I imagine the class would be for so long. And I always knew it was there, but I never labeled it as "vision."
—Andrea, high school English teacher

Teachers imagine what they could be doing in the classroom, how they could be interacting with their students, and what they and their students could be achieving. They envision classroom activities, discussions, and projects. They picture the kind of learning environment in which they and their students could work—including the design of the classroom, the type of school, and even the kind of community that would support their dreams. These images of ideal classroom practice are *teachers' visions*. They embody teachers' hopes for the future and play a significant role in their lives and work.

In describing his vision, Carlos, a high school history teacher, focuses upon the importance of educational access for Latinos like himself; he feels that academic success will contribute to the gradual improvement of the economic and political status of the Latino population in his community. He observes, "I've seen that education is the way that any community has improved in this country. Just looking through history it's been through education."

For teachers like Carlos, vision is more than a teaching philosophy. Vision is a set of vivid and concrete images of practice. Jake, a tenth-grade history teacher, explained that his vision "turns [my teaching ideas and philosophy] into *something real*." It instantiates what would happen "between 8 o'clock and 3 o'clock." As Jake put it, "You can look at it, you can point to it." Stella, a novice English teacher, explained,

> My vision is something tangible in a way that I can picture how my classroom will look and how my students will be and how I will be in my classroom. And my philosophy is more how I will get there. I don't think my philosophy is something I could reach and describe exactly . . . but vision . . . it's definitely something I . . . imagine in my mind.

Another teacher, Sarah, said simply, "Vision is what I see when I close my eyes. Philosophy is what is behind those ideas." Andrea remarked that, while her philosophy had developed recently, her vision had been something she had held for a long time, and that it had a different quality that was personal, emotional, and powerful: "This is my vision, [this] reflects a lot about how I *feel* about teaching. My philosophy is still developing, but *this* is something I've been carrying around for 7 years."

Although teachers' personal visions are substantial and concrete, they are largely unexplored. Andrea explained:

> In my [teacher education] program, that word had never been used, never introduced and never ever discussed. There were always "goals and expectations" but never the idea of vision. But I've seen in my head what I imagine the class would be for so long. And I always knew it was there, but I never labeled it as "vision."

This book is designed to explore teachers' visions. It draws upon surveys and interviews with a wide range of teachers (including novice and experienced teachers of elementary and middle school as well as of high school history, English, mathematics, and science) and focuses upon the development of four teachers—Andrea, Kelly, Jake, and Carlos—over an 9-year period. (For a discussion of the methods used in this study, see Appendix A; a copy of the survey is included in Appendix B.) For these teachers, vision represents what Maxine Greene (1988) describes as "a consciousness of possibility" (p. 23). Vision shapes the way that they feel about their teaching, their students and their school and helps to explain the changes they make in their classrooms, the choices they make in their teaching, and even the decisions they make about their futures as teachers. When they feel that their vision is within reach and they may be able to attain it, they feel successful and remain motivated, committed, and inspired in teaching. But when they believe that their vision is very far from what they are experiencing, they may come to doubt themselves, their schools, their students, and their future as teachers.

A MORE COMPLEX VIEW OF VISION

What former president George H. W. Bush famously termed "the vision thing" often evades precise definition. For the most part, however, vision in education has been viewed as institutional, future-oriented, positive, and rational.

From Organizational Vision to Personal Vision

Educational scholar Michael Fullan (1993) has observed that "few concepts are as misunderstood and misapplied" as vision (p. 28). In education, the emphasis has been almost exclusively upon organizational visions providing a focus that can inspire and guide groups and institutions. Great time and effort is spent crafting organizational missions or vision statements, and trying to get teachers to "buy into" them (Evans, 1996; Hargreaves, 1994; Louis & Miles, 1990). As one veteran mathematics teacher, Mari, told me, despite the fact that her school had undertaken multiple reform efforts including attempts to develop a school vision, none of them included asking teachers about their visions: "No one has ever asked me about that before…nobody ever listens to what matters." Yet from Fullan's perspective, teachers' personal vision—which "comes from within and gives meaning to their work"—serves as the foundation of powerful reform, and organizations ignore them at their peril (p. 13).

Vision Embodies the Past and the Present

Churchill is reputed to have commented, "The farther back you can look, the farther forward you are likely to see." His observation emphasizes the fact that imagination is about not only seeing into the future, but also of understanding the past. Yet, while vision has long been equated in popular thinking with the ability to understand the world as well as to foresee the future, researchers in education have concentrated primarily upon vision's implications for future planning. However, personal vision is as much about how we understand our past and present as it is about developing images of what could lie ahead.

In fact, while teachers' vision serves as a productive guide for future practice, it also provides a means of reflecting on past activities and experiences in the classroom. Like a mirror, teachers compare daily practice to their vision and recognize successes as well as identifying areas for improvement. In that sense, teachers' vision looks back and sees forward, encompassing past efforts in order to move closer to future aims.

Vision Can Have a Dark Side

Although philosophers, political leaders, and writers extol the virtues of vision, they also point to the dangers of the imagination and the blindness it can bring. For instance, the title character of the novel *Don Quixote* provides a particularly ambivalent image of a vision leading a dreamer astray. Quixote becomes so enamored by tales of knighthood that he creates an entire imaginary world, and the metaphor of Quixote's charging at windmills emphasizes the perils of becoming foolishly captivated by one's dreams.

In education, there is also the potential for visions to lead us astray. For instance, many teachers adopt ambitious and powerful visions to lead their change efforts. These can be profoundly motivating and inspiring. However, if their efforts fall short, teachers with such visions are subject to feelings of disillusionment and despair that can lead them to become jaded about the possible success of efforts in the future and in some cases to leave teaching altogether (Little, 1996). And, if teachers develop an overly grand vision of what their classroom should look like, which they cannot yet accomplish, the jarring tension between vision and real practice can cause teachers to feel deflated and discouraged, to lose confidence, and sometimes to become more conservative in their teaching (Austin, 1997; Hammerness, 1997; Moffett & Hammerness, 1998).

Visions can also be culturally biased or exclusionary. Teachers may have visions of the ideal classroom that do not allow for or accommodate a diverse student body. Furthermore, the limited vantage point of a teacher's own "apprenticeship of observation" can make it particularly difficult to develop or to imagine classrooms that work differently or resolve some of the problems of the classrooms they grew up in (Britzman, 1991; Lortie, 1975). In short, vision may make some teachers' ambitions soar, but vision can also perpetuate stereotypes and suppress alternative possibilities.

Vision Is Emotional

Aristotle argued that the physical act of vision enables us to distinguish among a variety of types of information that we observe in the external world—for him, vision was vital to thought and understanding. Yet he also felt that vision was not simply a means of understanding and argued that it provided an intimate conduit to the emotions, thoughts, actions, and experiences of others—in turn, providing insight into what it means to be human.

Similarly, more than just something that leads to or inspires emotions, teachers' personal vision is something deeply emotional in and of itself. Vision encompasses both positive and negative emotions, feelings such as care, passion, concern, or joy, as well as shame, guilt, and fear. Yet in most conventional discussions of vision, particularly with regards to organizational and school reform, it is often reduced to a set of cerebral, rationally produced plans.

One of the reasons that the emotional aspects of vision may be ignored is that feelings are believed to be separate from thinking and reasoning (Hargreaves, 1998). Many of us feel that emotions interfere with thinking, and we are more comfortable thinking about emotions as a way to set the stage for rational thinking. However, recent biological evidence presented by Damasio (1994) and Sacks (1995) suggest that emotions are critical to our decision making.

And in fact, much of the power of teachers' vision comes from the fusion of this kind of emotion with understanding. Vision brings together teachers' passions—their hopes, cares, and dreams—with their understandings—their knowledge about how and what children should be learning.

Looking to the Future and Learning from the Past

Seeing vision as institutional, future-oriented, rational, and positive is far too simplistic. As the visions of the teachers in this book suggest, vision is deeply personal. It can look to the past and the present as well as the future. It can inspire and motivate, but it can also lead to problems. For these teachers, vision functions both as a means of looking forward to what they want to do and back to what they have been doing. It can be positive and inspiring or problematic and depressing, particularly if their ideal is very far from their current practice. And in the process it shapes their view of themselves as successful or unsuccessful and influences their professional decisions, particularly about when to stay, where to go, and whether to leave teaching altogether.

TWO CENTRAL STRUGGLES

While this book focuses on teachers' vision, it is as much about how teachers navigate and address two longstanding tensions in teaching: maintaining the delicate balance between constantly shifting demands of subject matter and students' needs; and dealing with the uneasy tension between their ideals and their current practice.

Balancing Subject and Students

Why is this tension important? These two central elements—teachers' views of students and teachers' views of their subjects—help determine what teachers aim for in the classroom and how they evaluate their success. Yet keeping those two elements in balance is difficult. On the one hand, if all students aren't introduced to the central topics, problems, and issues of the disciplines, they will never attain the levels of understanding or performance that many people think are required for a successful life. On the other hand, not all students have the same exposure to or preparation for reaching such high levels. If teachers try to meet students at the level of preparation, they run the risk of not aiming high enough. However, if they focus only on the standards of their profession and the key ideas in their subject area, they may discourage students or fail to provide students with the support and structure needed to be successful.

Scaffolding important!

Teachers' visions can help reveal how teachers conceive of their subjects and their students, and how much attention they pay to each. For some teachers, their visions focus upon their students. For instance, high school science teacher Kelly's vision is filled with images of students—students discussing their work with their peers and with her, asking questions, doing research, making connections to real-world issues of science. But for others, like Andrea, the emphasis is upon the subject matter. When Andrea describes her vision, she emphasizes the material she imagines her students reading and discussing and thinking about—even down to the details of particular texts and topics.

In either case, focusing on only one half of the equation— students or subject matter—can lead to problems. For instance, Lily, a novice sixth-grade mathematics teacher, imagined a class driven by purposeful investigations in mathematics with students engaging in sophisticated explorations into numbers in the real world. Yet she described a "huge disconnect" between her vision for mathematical activities and what her middle school students could do–they were not yet able to do the kind of mathematical thinking she imagined. She said that her lack of success in the classroom and her inability to carry out her vision was "so depressing that I decided it was much better to just . . . work all the time and not think about it." She explained,

> If I stop and think about it, I'm satisfied with pieces of my teaching, but there's so much more that I should and could be doing. I guess my vision reflects what I think my teaching should be and how kids learn. And I'm not there. Which means I'm not doing everything I can to help kids learn.

Another new teacher, Sarah, had a vision of students working as authors together in small groups, or "learning communities," with a strong focus upon the process of writing. But only 6 months into her intern teaching year in elementary school, she said her hopes had been so badly dashed that she described her vision as "trashed." Although Sarah's ideals for her students were powerful and exciting, she couldn't figure out an appropriate way for her students to engage in those kinds of activities that would reflect their readiness and their current capabilities.

If teachers like Lily focus much of their vision on their subject matter, they may overlook students' capabilities, needs, and interests. On the other hand, teachers like Sarah may focus much of their vision upon what they hope and dream for their students and may lose sight of the ways in which they want students to develop in their disciplines.

For teachers like Lily and Sarah, the experience of comparing their visions for their disciplines with the needs of their students, or their visions for their students with the demands of the discipline can prompt feelings of discouragement and despair. Those teachers seek reasons to explain their disappointing assessment, at times blaming themselves, the school, or, perhaps worse, their students and the communities in which they teach. Even more worrisome, these teachers learn to discount their visions, to doubt themselves and to question their students' capacities. Lily explained that she had come to learn not to expect as much as she had hoped from herself or her students. She said she was still trying to attain her vision, but "I don't see it as a requirement . . . I also learned to lower my expectations in the first month of my teaching."

But by examining their visions and expanding their visions to address both subject matter and students, teachers can find ways to balance where they want students to go with where students are. For the teachers in this book, navigating this tension is no easy matter, but it lies at the heart of their efforts to improve their practice and to sustain themselves and their passion for teaching.

Bridging the Gap Between Vision and Practice

Why is this tension important? Many people are drawn into teaching because they see it as a noble profession, and they have powerful visions regarding what they hope to accomplish in that work. They aim to be successful, not only through their own students and making a difference in those children's lives, but also (at least for some teachers) through improving society in some way. However, it is well known that the first years of teaching can bring a kind of "reality shock" (Veenman, 1984) regarding the difficulty of achieving those kinds of goals, particularly in school contexts that are poorly funded and have few resources. Yet many teachers manage not only to survive but also to succeed in these challenging circumstances. These teachers have learned to navigate the gap between their ideals and dreams and the kinds of instruction, activities, and achievements their context seems to support. Indeed, it is not simply the context that determines the ways in which teachers are able to teach, but the ability to bridge the gap between vision and what they are able to do in their current context that defines how teachers feel about their work and how inspired they feel.

For the teachers in this book, vision functions as what Jake called a "measuring stick" that can indicate how far current practice sits from where one wants to be. Teachers can reflect upon their daily work and current context in light of their vision. For those who feel that the distance between their vision and current context is reasonable and navigable, evaluating practice in the light of vision invites feelings of motivation and fulfillment. For instance, Kelly explained that she felt that although her school site was not ideal, the gap between her current context and her vision was not so vast as to be insurmountable. She said that she felt that she could maintain progress toward her vision and said that "the thought of me progressing toward this vision is what has kept me in teaching." Patricia, a biology teacher, explained that her vision felt close enough that it kept her motivated and committed. She commented that her vision "keep[s] me going!" She explained that trying to find new ways to attain her vision led her to new learning, which in turn fueled her motivation and initiated the cycle again, explaining that "I'm learning so much about how to get further" that her sense of movement toward her vision helps keep her in teaching. When teachers like Kelly and Patricia feel like the gap is reasonable, they can recognize small successes, appreciate their own growth, and identify accomplishments in relationship to their visions. Those teachers feel inspired to reflect upon past practice and to evaluate their strengths and weaknesses.

Yet for those who feel that the gap between vision and what they are able to do in their current context is too vast, the distance can lead to tension, doubt, disappointment, and feelings of failure. Lily, who felt that her vision of her math students was extremely far from what she was able to do in her current context, referred to her vision disparagingly as "dreamland" and "an uneducated ideal." Sarah, who also felt a great gap between vision and what she was able to do in her practice, observed, "Your ideas get so far away from what you are dealing with every day that you end up distrusting what you visualized." She said that this gap had led to feelings of profound discouragement: "I like to overcome obstacles, but this one I cannot overcome. I give up. Whatever illusions [I had] of helping or changing or affecting students' lives. . . . There's no way, it's physically impossible to do it." Felicity, also a student teacher, said simply, "on an emotional level, it's really difficult to keep going."

Ironically, if these teachers' visions weren't so clear, they might not feel so far away from them. They would not be striving for some ideal, but they might be better able to maintain a sense of satisfaction and comfort with their work. Instead, the teachers with strong clear visions who saw a huge gap between what they *wanted* to do and what they *were able* to do in their current context were those who were already thinking about leaving teaching or, at the very least, switching schools. Sarah said that she was leaving the public elementary school where she was teaching at the end of the year because she was "not going to make it here. . . . [I'm] not going to be able to do this year after year." Felicity remarked that "there's really days when I am just depressed to be at that school. I hate to go there. And that can really interfere . . . not with my desire to teach but maybe my motivation to keep going." All three of these teachers—Sarah, Lily, and Felicity—were planning to switch schools at the end of the school year.

This turnover of teachers, which Ingersoll (2001) calls "migration," is a growing problem exacerbating the shortage of teachers that exists in some communities. Ingersoll has found that nearly one-half of teacher attrition can be accounted for by exodus to different schools. Not surprisingly, such movement is concentrated in schools and districts in low-socioeconomic communities (such as those in which Sarah and Felicity were teaching) which are experiencing an increasing and steady loss of teachers (Haycock, 2000; Lankford, Loeb, & Wyckoff, 2002). Teachers rarely remain at one school long enough to get to know their students and the community, or even fellow teachers. This is also particularly problematic for reforming schools that may seek to develop a cadre of teachers who are committed to sustaining long-term change efforts (Moffett, 1999).

Often rewards and incentives are offered as a means to address this problem. But where teachers choose to go may in large part be determined not just by pay and other benefits, but by where teachers believe they may be successful (Johnson & Birkeland, 2002). And whether teachers feel efficacious may in large part be determined by whether they are making progress toward their ideals and feel closer to enacting their vision of good practice.

CHAPTER 2

Teaching with the Subject in Mind

Andrea and I are sitting together at noon on a warm day in late May. The sun is shining through the big glass windows in her classroom and we can hear the voices of several students outside on the lawn beneath the windows, eating their lunches. Andrea has just finished reading several scenes from *Romeo and Juliet* with two classes of ninth-grade students. She has been reflecting upon what she did that day, and I ask her about some comments she made in a previous discussion about possibly leaving teaching following her first year as a full-time teacher. Andrea responds that she has been struggling with that question. Currently, she is considering jobs at other schools, wondering whether perhaps she still does want to teach but perhaps "just not here" at Jefferson High School.[1] However, she feels quite guilty about leaving Jefferson:

> At the same time, I keep thinking, well, if I have the choice I should be teaching in a place like this because maybe this is where kids need me the most and where I feel like maybe I could make a difference. But I feel like I'm not making a difference. And so I don't know if maybe that was part guilt, saying, since I can't do it, well, I just shouldn't do it at all.

In addition, Andrea contends with pressure from her father and her fiancé, who both seem to be hinting to her that she is "wasting [her] intelligence and [her] life doing this." She explains that she is feeling particularly depressed lately:

> Even though people keep reassuring me that, "well, don't get discouraged" . . . I just had progress reports and I have 55% of my students failing right now. And it's not enough that the other English teachers are saying, "I've been here 25 years and it's been the same way

ever since I've been here. I always have 50% of my kids failing. It's not you, it's them."

Andrea reflects, "And that's okay and maybe that will be okay for half an hour, but then I think, 'Well, no, that's not okay with me.' "

For many educators, this conversation may signal the beginning of a familiar story: a new teacher, placed in a classroom of diverse children with intense and complex needs, begins to question her commitment to teaching—or at least her ability to make a difference in such classrooms. Will Andrea's story end with the familiar conclusion of a disheartened teacher choosing to leave the profession? What will happen to Andrea's commitment to teaching and to her students? What conclusions will she draw about her ability to make a difference and about her vision, and how will she feel about them?

Andrea's vision reveals a focus upon a shared intellectual investigation of literature, with the teacher playing the role of guide, source of knowledge, and inspiration, and the students as very active seekers of knowledge and understanding. But what really stands out is the focus in her vision upon her subject matter. For Andrea, what really mattered was teaching students to read and interpret literature. Her vision concentrated upon images of students engaged in sophisticated literary discussions, analyzing classic and noncanonical texts together, searching for universal themes about love, life, death, romance, friendship, and family. Even as a student teacher, Andrea had already thought deeply about the types of interpretive skills she imagined her students honing as they worked with her and even imagined in detail the particular novels, plays, and poetry the students would read as they encountered profound universal themes for the first time. Like many teachers, Andrea found great joy in and felt considerable passion for her subject matter, and she noted that her love for her discipline played a key role in her decision to teach (Huberman, 1993). In fact, Andrea noted that in addition to considering a teaching career, she had also briefly thought about becoming a writer or journalist—anything to allow her to pursue her love for language and literature. Ultimately she had chosen teaching, in part because her own experience in school as a student of literature had been so positive and important to her personal development. Andrea's emphasis upon her subject is typical of a number of teachers in this study for whom subject matter was central to their vision. Kelly, for instance, described her role in her vision as "the human representative of her subject matter," and Gary reiterated again and again that economics was the centerpiece of his vision.

Yet for Andrea and for the other teachers like her with an emphasis upon subject, what she learns about teaching (and whether or not she maintains her commitment to it) depends upon how she deals with the tension between subject matter and students in her vision. Andrea's first few years teaching could suggest that for her (and teachers like her) it can be particularly problematic to consider subject matter and students in opposition. It seems to leave such teachers with an untenable choice between lowering expectations for students and sticking to standards that seem impossible to reach. But Andrea's thinking about students and subject begin to come into balance, suggesting that over time, she has been able to resolve some of the difficult questions around what is appropriate for her students and what she dreams they can learn.

At the same time that her concern for subject matter shapes her development, her context is also crucial. On the one hand, Andrea can control her expectations of herself, her students, and her teaching by lowering or raising her standards and stay at her current school. On the other hand, she can move to a different school—as she does after her first year. Yet simply moving does not resolve the problem, because she again will have to balance her own ideals and her expectations of what students can accomplish.

ANDREA'S VISION

In response to my question prompts, Andrea wrote a description of her vision while she was a student teacher. She began by talking about the physical space of her ideal classroom, about which she was quite specific. The walls are "a bit old" and even the wallpaper has aged—"what was once optic white is now a dullish and soothing yellow." "Bookshelves span one part of the walls and . . . large beautiful windows look out onto green trees and lovely fields." No desks are in this room; rather, in the center is a round table. This is the heart of the room and of the activity. "This is where the students sit to face each other and the teacher in a roundtable discussion." One teacher's desk graces a corner of the room and the "eyes of dead poets" depicted in various posters look down at the students. This environment, Andrea suggests, fosters learning without even requiring anyone to speak or act. She follows this description of the physical space with the comment that "learning has already begun."

Andrea saw herself playing multiple roles in her ideal classroom. She is "teacher, leader, purveyor of knowledge, confidante, friend, inspiration, guide." Her physical level was important in this classroom; Andrea sits at the table with them, as she views it, "seeing eye to eye, mind to mind." Andrea does not "sound on through long lectures" but rather provides "short, informative minilectures on sociohistorical context of the particular novel being studied."

From the students she envisioned "loads of classroom participation." She explained that she wants to "learn from my students," commenting that "I want to know what they see and feel and believe." Ideally, Andrea does not tell them what to think; rather, she "elicits interpretations from them before offering my own." She suggested the metaphor of investigators to illustrate the work of the class: "We take apart the text together—delving through the passages of the text like bold investigators—searching for treasures and truth." Students' roles are to think critically and interpret the text as a community.

> They are engaging in dialogue, challenging themselves and each other to go deeper, look harder to find the answers—the answers to their own questions—if perhaps to life's greater dilemmas as dealt with through literature. They are referring to specific pages, explaining the design of the novel, interpreting imagery, becoming poets themselves. They must search to find something in it for themselves, to reveal to me what it means to them to be navigators, and poets, and young thinkers.

Andrea sees literature as a lens for self-inquiry and understanding: to better understand responses to "life's dilemmas" to which literature has provided multiple responses. In fact, Andrea explained that in this ideal classroom students will learn to "find the beauty in language, how to analyze and interpret it, to understand it, use it, play with it, hear it, write it." She envisioned teaching specific texts, novels such as Morrison's *Beloved,* or Faulkner's *Light in August,* and poetry by Sylvia Plath, Langston Hughes, Maya Angelou, and T. S. Eliot. Andrea believes that such texts will prompt student questions and inquiry, and will challenge them and inspire them to explore topics such as love, death, female identity, sexuality, history, conquest, and failure. As she sees it, these texts will "challenge and inspire these students as much as possible to make their lives richer and fuller."

Andrea imagined her ideal classroom as providing a counter to what she views as the "techno-chaos" of current society, and as educating students to be sensitive, insightful, and creative thinkers:

> I would love to create and inspire young poets/writers and to encourage their place and their significance in the world. In a world rapidly advancing into "techno-chaos" we need to remember and return to the power of the word, of poetry and language and feelings, and teach students to use their gifts and their imaginations to forge a movement toward a highly literate and sensitive society.

Like some teachers interviewed as part of this work, Andrea explained that her vision derived from her own past as a student. She noted that her vision was "pretty much taken all from my high school experience." Andrea's own experience of being a student in schools, what Lortie (1975) called the "apprenticeship of observation," was deeply influential in shaping her vision for her own future classroom.

ENCOUNTERING THE GAP BETWEEN VISION AND PRACTICE

While Andrea had long imagined engaging her students in sophisticated and passionate discussions about English literature, she had not thought as deeply about who her students might be and what they might be able to do. This knowledge about subject, but not students, contributed in large degree to the considerable gap between vision and practice that Andrea experienced as a student teacher, and then as a first-year teacher at Jefferson High School.

An Unrealistic Vision?

When I talked to Andrea the first time, right after she had completed her student-teaching year at Jefferson, she explained that she felt that her vision was extremely far from her practice. "I was being very idealistic," she said. She added that when she wrote her vision statement (in the middle of her student-teaching year), she was in the process of realizing that she was not currently able to attain the vision at Jefferson. It was "an unrealistic vision for me right now." She said that if I had asked her about the possibility of living this vision at the beginning of her student-teaching year, she might have felt more optimistic; but now, she was beginning to sense that the vision was impossible. "I would have thought, at that point, 'Oh, I could probably find this somewhere.' And [now] I don't think that I will."

Andrea felt that two aspects of her school constrained her ability to carry out the vision. First, "money was sort of an issue" in that she couldn't purchase the texts she wanted and she didn't have access to the kinds of books she wanted students to read. The lack of funds "completely limited the possibility of whatever I could take from here [indicating her vision statement] to put into my current situation."

But more important, the students she was teaching were not as well prepared nor as academically motivated as she had expected. She felt unprepared for the backgrounds, experiences, and apparent aspirations of her students, explaining that she was realizing that "most of the students are not college bound right now. . . . And so that certainly changed how I taught the material I did." She commented with surprise and dismay, "I didn't realize how low skills would be, just like awfully low." She concluded, "And so that, more than anything, limited my ideal vision, because their needs were so different from what I wanted to do." Her perception of the low skills and abilities of Jefferson students made her feel that she could not teach the literature she had envisioned. She described how drastically she had to change her curriculum when she realized that she could not "teach things I wanted to teach":

> And so the things that I had planned to do, I had to completely change. And the first 20 minutes of the first day, I realized that I could not teach things I wanted to teach. . . . And so that's one thing I don't think I could fully get into this year was the fact that it was reading. I couldn't get into teaching the literature that I love, teaching novels, which is what I love.

Andrea's struggle with the gap between vision and practice led her to some productive thinking. She explained that she began to recognize that her vision was built in large part upon her own experience as a student. Through her interactions with her students, she began to identify the potential limitations of a vision that was so connected to her own personal history and that might not reflect what was good or appropriate for other people. This insight began to contribute to some growing questions about ways in which her vision might not be appropriate for students unlike herself, and to some initial explorations regarding how she might adjust and shape it so that it was more about her students and less about her own interests.

Yet her experience of the gap also led her to some more difficult and troubling questions and conclusions. For instance, during that first interview, Andrea explained that she had begun to question whether the range of her vision was so narrow that it might only be appropriate for students just like herself, students attending a small private school. Perhaps it was even only possible in her own high school: "Even if I had a great situation, I still don't think I would ever achieve this, unless maybe I went back to teach in my high school," she commented. She was quite critical of what she termed her "ridiculous" reliance on the past, "I mean *this* [indicating her description of her vision], I think I was limiting myself then and being totally unrealistic."

The disappointment apparent in her comments echo the grief and even anger expressed by other teachers whom I interviewed, like Lily and Sarah, who also held distant visions and were teaching in unsupportive contexts. Sarah explained that in her current circumstances at her school she had trouble even recalling her vision: "What happens is you get blocked even thinking of what you can do because you have gotten so used to not being able to do things . . . it's sort of like when everything goes wrong. You are just trying to maintain." She concluded, "So I wouldn't really say that I am going to hold out for my vision."

Indeed, only 9 months into student teaching (perhaps also distrusting what she envisioned), Andrea had begun to wonder whether she should abandon her vision. She mentioned that she was interviewing at other schools. She noted that she was not even sure she should try to look for a place where she could attain her vision, because it was so depressing to feel unable to accomplish her vision: "What I'm looking for now—I'm trying to find a school, not so much where I can fulfill this vision, but somewhere I think I'll be happy." She added:

> Instead of looking into the past for what would work, in terms of the classroom, even though this [vision] would be my ideal, I'm thinking that I need to move away from this and think about what their needs are and what I need to change in the future for myself.

Even more worrisome, this experience of the gap between vision and reality was leading Andrea to question her initial belief that all students can learn. She wondered in private whether children in this low-income community might even have the capacity to accomplish what she had hoped for them.

Calibrations and Adjustments: "I have to adapt . . . I have to have flexible vision"

Andrea's efforts to bridge the considerable gap between her vision and her practice prompted considerable doubt and unease for her. Comparing the experience she and her students were having every day in class to what she had envisioned, was not only deeply unsettling but also dispiriting. Felicity, another young English teacher in similar circumstances, explained that she was so discouraged that "there were a lot of points when I just said I don't want to teach anymore."

The significant gap led Andrea to try to understand what was wrong. At varying times during these first two years she located the problem in different places—her vision, her teaching, her students, her school. Each selection prompted a different reaction; Andrea at various times experienced them all. Thinking that her vision or her students might be the problem, yet feeling at the same time that she could not abandon her vision entirely, compelled Andrea to calibrations. She shifted, stretched, and reconsidered her vision to meet the needs of her students and her vision.

Yet by her second year, now hired as a full-time first-year teacher at Jefferson High, Andrea explained that rather than abandon her vision, she had broadened its range. Instead of considering her vision as only possible at her alma mater or a similar private school, she was beginning to recognize that perhaps it could happen at a place like Jefferson. As she explained,

> I really thought my ideal was finding a place like where I'd gone to high school and I know we talked about that. And now I really don't think that necessarily that would be my ideal. Like it would be great, but I

think that having seen that I can make this [vision] work at a place like Jefferson makes me think that wherever I go, I can pretty much create my ideal classroom.

Andrea noted that in order to broaden the range of her vision—to imagine how it could be appropriate for her Jefferson students—she had to shift the vision in particular ways. She mused, "It just means that I have to adapt—like I have to have flexible vision. . . . I think in terms of my vision meeting the students' needs." She explained that she decided she might do better to teach novels that were not as sophisticated, so that her students might experience literature's benefits without struggling through complex language or intricate plot lines. She described this as "adjusting" her vision.

And so all the texts that I put in here [indicating her vision statement], in terms of things that I would ideally like to teach, didn't happen at all. But that's OK. I still tried to find things that were relevant to them. I think that was something too that I had to adjust.

Even though she was adjusting her vision, Andrea still felt that she was faithful to it and had been able to figure out how to enact her vision in a way that was reasonable for her students. She believed that she maintained her commitment to the focus of her vision, such as deep engagement in literature and an environment of inspiration, trust, and warmth.

I want to create that same feeling [as was at my private school]. For example, being the inspiration for my students. My students really engaging in the literature they're reading, feeling inspired by it. The confidence they feel, the warmth, the security of the classroom, that kind of thing. I still strive for that . . . the overall feeling I try to create in my classroom, that's still something that's taken from the vision.

She remarked that "the basic foundation pieces" of her vision have remained the same—"freedom and confidence and freedom of expression" even when she has altered it to meet their needs.

At the same time, Andrea also described ways in which she had watered down the vision. For instance, she no longer specified the texts that she originally did. She told me she was realizing that rather than read authors like Toni Morrison and Faulkner, her students were better able to understand texts like *To Kill a Mockingbird*. She said that now her ideal vision would be that "students felt that what we were studying, whatever it was, that they were in some way learning about themselves." Even while she was describing ways that she had adjusted her vision, Andrea emphasized that her vision hadn't really changed. "I think I'll always have this vision. . . . if I had different students, maybe I could take a little bit more from here [indicating vision statement]. I don't know that it would change very much." She concluded, "I still think this is my vision [but] again, I need to think of their needs more than mine. This [vision] would fulfill my needs but not necessarily the needs of my students." Other teachers in similar circumstances found themselves making the same kind of adjustments and tuning. Lily said that she had come to learn not to expect as much as she had hoped: "I think I'm still moving toward it [my vision] but I don't set it as a requirement. I also learned to lower my expectations in my first month of teaching."

Talking about adjustments and calibrations may seem abstract and ambiguous to some, but for Andrea, the experience of tuning her vision to her students' needs, capabilities, and ambitions represented a daily and concrete challenge, as well as one that called up considerable questions, doubts, and fears. In her practice, Andrea tried to effect a balance between challenging and pushing her students toward the kind of academic and intellectual experiences she dreamed of—asking them to write sonnets, involving them in the reading of a difficult play. At the same time, as shown in the narrative of her practice that follows, Andrea found herself "filling in" some of the rich discussion she dreams of (for instance, rather than asking Luis or another student to expand his ideas about Romeo's risk taking in the garden, she talked about it herself). Andrea did much of the talking in this discussion, while students occasionally filled in with one or two word responses to her questions.

A PICTURE OF PRACTICE: TEACHING *ROMEO AND JULIET*

A few minutes before class starts, Andrea enters a little breathless having rushed back to her classroom from substituting for another teacher in the other building. She explains that she is frequently asked to take classes for absent teachers across the yard; it makes her days particularly hectic. She piles a stack of papers on her desk and sits down, taking a notebook out. Scanning the room, she begins checking students as absent or present.

Students are taking their seats in the rows of desks that face her desk and my table. A group of three boys, George, Carter, and Foster, and a girl, Julie, are talking to one another about a movie they'd seen, while another boy, LaRoy, has taken out a book and is reading quietly. One student takes a seat and says, "I'm not sure I did the sonnet right." Andrea assures her, "That's OK, Lupe, I'm sure you did better than you think." The bell rings and about 18 of the 25 desks in the room are filled. A small stepladder sits in the front of the room, right in front of Andrea's desk.

Andrea asks the students to take out the sonnets that they had written the night before. Kareem calls out, "It was hard." Andrea responds, "I know, my sixth-period class made me do one!" She then asks, "How many of you tried to do a sonnet last night?" Most students raise their hands. Did anyone want to share his or her sonnet? Francisco says, "no." "Doesn't anyone want to share, not even one person?" The students fidget with their papers. Andrea walks around and collects the poems from the students. She remarks, "I'm glad you all tried it. Was the hardest part doing the stressed and unstressed syllables?" Stephanie volunteers, "I just worried about trying to find the right words and having them match."

Andrea explains that she is going to pick one student's sonnet at random and read it, anonymously. She selects a piece of paper from the pile she had collected and begins to read; the poem by a female student asking another to be her "boyfriend." A few students clap when Andrea finishes reading it. Some call out names, trying to guess who wrote it: "Brandy!" "Jennifer!" "Venus!" Three male students call out, "Read another." Andrea selects one about a recent basketball game and the merits of the winning team. "This poem is coming straight from my head," it begins. The last line is: "The very last thing I want to say is I hope my poem deserves a good 'A.'" Andrea remarks that it is very good and that she could really hear the stressed and unstressed syllables in the poem.

Andrea explains to the class that she had given the assignment for two reasons. First, she wanted them to understand the intricacy of the language of Shakespeare and to understand the difficulty and "the genius" it took to write these plays. Second, she wanted her students to have an opportunity to exercise their creativity. She urges them, as they continued to read the play, to keep their own attempts as poets in mind and to "continue to look at the language."

Andrea then remarks, "OK, what we are going to do is a little different today: the balcony scene is a major scene in the play. What it means for Romeo and Juliet is important, they declare their love for each other. But it is also important in terms of *character*. You should pay close attention to what Romeo says and what it suggests about his character, and to what Juliet says and what it suggests about her character. Because they each have a different perspective on the relationship and you can see it in the language they use." Andrea points out that it was "significant" that Juliet was up on the balcony, "up above" Romeo. It underscores the way Romeo puts Juliet on a pedestal, she adds.

Two girls, Stephanie and Rachel, volunteer to play Juliet. "OK, we need Romeo," Andrea explains. No one volunteered, but a number of students called out one another's names. "Lenny!" "Juan!" Several students remark that a girl could be Romeo if she wanted. Andrea urges the boys to volunteer, noting that, "some of you need extra credit." The students want to know how much and Andrea says 10 points. Luis volunteers: "OK, I'll do it."

Rachel steps up the ladder that Andrea has pulled in front of Luis's desk. Luis sits on his desk, swinging his legs. Andrea gives some background for the scene. "All right, in this scene, Juliet is not immediately aware of Romeo. She is just talking to herself at first and doesn't know he's there."

Luis, still kicking his legs back and forth, reads the first few lines, when Romeo first spies Juliet at her balcony. "It is the east and Juliet is the sun!" He obligingly reads along for a while, occasionally stumbling on some words, and then Andrea stops him. She asks, "What does Romeo compare Juliet's eyes to?" Luis says, "The twinkling of the stars." Andrea asks Luis why that comparison is a compliment? "She's so beautiful!" he responds. Andrea agrees and adds that Romeo also means that Juliet is "celestial." Andrea points out that Romeo is using all kinds of "unrealistic" and supernatural beings as metaphors for Juliet. During this time, the other students are quiet—some watching, some with their heads down on their desks.

The two students read a few more paragraphs of text. Andrea stops them with a wave of her hand and asks Luis what Romeo is comparing Juliet to now. "An angel," he responds. Andrea notes that Romeo is again comparing Juliet to "otherworldly" things, and that he is being "unrealistic" in how he talks about her. The students continue to read a bit more. "Juliet" reads the part in which she urges Romeo to "deny thy father and refuse thy name." Andrea again stops the reading and asks the class, "So what is she asking him to do?" A student questions, "She is asking why his name is Romeo?" Andrea agrees, "Well, yes, but what is she asking him to do?" No one responds immediately and Andrea explains, "The whole fact that he is a Montague is a great distress . . . it will really cause trouble." She explains that Juliet is asking him to give up his name and thus his familial association.

The class continues in this way until a few minutes before the period ends, when Andrea thanks the two students who read, and asks for volunteers for the next scene for tomorrow. Andrea calls out a reminder to do their homework, adding, "OK, we'll finish this on Tuesday! Thanks for reading, those of you who did!"

Even while she made adjustments, Andrea did not assume that she was necessarily responding to the gap between vision and practice in the "right" way. She continued to wonder and worry about the nature of her adjustments. Was she being fair to herself and her vision? Was her vision appropriate? Was she being fair to her students? Could her students accomplish the vision? Indeed, her investment in both her students *and* her vision put her in a particularly difficult position. Was she ultimately sacrificing one for the other? And which one was ultimately losing out?

Because of these difficult struggles, she sought reasons to help her understand the gap she was experiencing between vision and practice. Thus, at times, she wondered whether it was not the qualities in her students, but perhaps her own teaching that contributed to the gap between vision and practice. She noted unhappily, "I still have more than half of my students fail." Andrea refused to shift the blame for her students' failure. She declared that it was her responsibility to figure out how to teach her students well and to get closer to her vision. As she asserted, she came to believe that the lack of success of her students was "not okay with me." Thus the gap between her vision and her reality also led her to feel guilty and disappointed in herself and to doubt her own abilities as a teacher:

> My ideal classroom is that higher level thinking, that analysis, that interpretation . . . and it's difficult for me, and I suppose, you know, I blame myself. We did some poetry earlier in the year, and some of them still have a lot of trouble with interpretation and looking at language. And I blame myself . . . what I'm supposed to be teaching them is how to interpret and if they're still not doing it, then I obviously fell short somewhere.

It may have been productive and important that vision made Andrea uncomfortable with circumstances such as the high failure rate of her students that other teachers urged her to accept. Yet it is also clear that the gap between vision and practice led her to feel guilty, to doubt her own abilities and (as she repeats) to "blame" herself. Andrea received little help from her colleagues at Jefferson in thinking about these matters. While several teachers would occasionally share some worksheets or materials, Andrea rarely had opportunities to talk with them about teaching or the students. She said she never would have talked about her vision with them, as she worried they might not have agreed. Or worse, they might have told her she was too idealistic. While she often voiced a longing for like-minded colleagues, Andrea said she did not mind the lack of communication with her current peers because she felt that her fellow teachers would not necessarily share her vision. Furthermore, she was dismayed by her colleagues' apparent acceptance of the failure rate of their students, and she questioned whether developing a relationship with her fellow teachers would be productive or helpful for her own development. However, the lack of collegial support also meant that Andrea had to wrestle with her concerns, fears, doubts, and nagging worries on her own.

Thus, at still other times, her school context loomed preeminent. At those times, Andrea wondered whether she could perhaps enact her vision if she were in a school similar to her own alma mater. Those questions led her to consider leaving Jefferson for a school more similar to her own private school.

Indeed, the gap that guided teachers like Kelly and Jake to productively and purposefully analyze their practice, seeking innovative means of reaching their vision, contributed to a very different experience for Andrea. What Andrea felt was not motivation and inspiration, but doubt, discouragement, and guilt. What she (and other teachers who also experienced a significant gap between vision and practice) learned from the gap was not a series of fresh approaches to the vision, but that something was terribly wrong. Teachers I interviewed who described a similarly vast gap also talked about feeling as if their vision perhaps was not possible anywhere. Their disappointment is jarringly apparent in their discussions of their experiences. As another preservice teacher, Felicity, said passionately: "I was so heartbroken . . . it's just very hard to keep motivated every day for your students. I am depressed . . . I see how it's already wearing on me and we're not even halfway through the year. I either need to make a change in where I'm teaching or change professions completely."

In fact, despite some of the gains Andrea felt she had made with regard to her students at Jefferson and despite the fondness she had for her students there, she made a decision to leave Jefferson at the end of the year, and began to look for jobs in private schools. She chose a job teaching English at St. Mark's, a private school in a suburban community not far from where she lived. She looked forward to finally being able to accomplish her vision in a place that shared many similarities with her own experience in private school.

THE IDEAL CONTEXT FOR VISION?
TEACHING AT ST. MARK'S

By moving to St. Mark's, Andrea had chosen to teach in a school that offered many of the features that were consistent with her vision. St. Mark's is a religious boys' school, serving approximately 400 students (who are 62% Caucasian, 15% Hispanic, 12% Asian, 6% African American, and 5% Pacific Islander), and it offered opportunities to work with a small close-knit faculty. St. Mark's is well respected both for its athletics and its academics. It sends about 94% of its students on to college every year, many of whom attend state and University of California programs.

Such a school context might seem ideal for Andrea, meeting many of the features she had initially imagined as part of her vision. She noted, "I love the school environment; there was so much more support and collegiality," and she praised the "incredible sense of community." She commented that (in contrast to the Jefferson faculty) the St. Mark's faculty was especially "supportive, eager to help, and open and giving." She described some students as "incredibly bright," capable students, but added that the image of St. Mark's as "only taking the elite" was incorrect. She felt that St. Mark's accepted a range of students that may even have been more diverse than Jefferson's.

And yet Andrea's first year at St. Mark's, she reflected, was in many ways one of the hardest yet. By the end of her first year, she said she contemplated leaving teaching even more seriously than she had the previous year while teaching at Jefferson. Andrea had taught several sections of English literature, and as she put it, "I had a really horrible class and really questioned if I could go back the next year." She had been asked to take over another teacher's class of seniors and she noted it was "really a struggle." Their behavior was "awful," and the students and she had not seemed to accomplish anything in terms of learning. She had to create an individual study plan for each student, and even that had not worked.

Andrea noted that at the end of the year she was "left with an awful feeling": she felt ashamed of what she had *not* accomplished, and discouraged about her ability to teach and about the impossibility of attaining her vision. As at Jefferson, Andrea again repeated, "I blame myself—a lot went wrong." She reflected, "I really thought I could have this vision, and it won't be too hard to achieve it." Like many others, Andrea had assumed that if she taught in a supportive school context, her ability to teach in the way she had dreamed and to enact her vision would be immediately possible.

However, Andrea reflected that this experience began to help her learn more about her students. As at Jefferson, she began to focus upon her students and their learning. Her vision of her students began to take on more texture. She explained that at Jefferson and even at St. Mark's her vision of children was based upon assumptions about their motivations and needs. She had continued to imagine students in her vision as just like her. They would share her passion for literature, for intellectual conversation, and they would be prepared to engage in the kind of academic work that she envisioned. She had still taken for granted the belief that "all kids would be highly motivated" (as she herself had been as a high school student). As her first St. Mark's students were a class of seniors, she had assumed that they would be mature and, with college on the horizon for them, able to take a long-term perspective. She says she also believed that her students would all automatically be interested in what she was teaching.

She reflected that this vision was deeply shaped by her own experience as a student, rather than by who her students actually were. Yet the experience of learning more about what her students needed and what they were interested in and able to accomplish was extremely valuable: "It ended up being a good thing." As she explained, "my vision of the ideal student, my vision of kids" had developed and deepened. Rather than a vision of herself as the model for her ideal student, it developed into a vision of what these students could look like, need, contribute, and accomplish.

She explained that this more complex and differentiated vision of students vastly increased her ability to teach them well. She felt that she no longer made assumptions about them. She noted, "Now the first thing I assume is not that they are lazy [when they aren't doing work] but that something is going on." She also noted that she was learning to appreciate even more the importance of knowing about the contexts and backgrounds of kids' lives: "More and more I realize how kids struggle and that their capacity to learn depends upon their home life." Andrea noted that she was beginning to feel more "responsible for them" in terms of "caring for them" and "knowing about their lives." She also explained that she now feels more and more comfortable asking kids about how they are doing and what is going on with them.

And, as Andrea learned more about her students' needs and backgrounds, she began to recognize and appreciate the importance of making connections between her curriculum and her students' own lives: "I find myself doing things that are more relevant to them—more and more I encourage my kids to ask why we are doing this, why it is important. I find myself trying to identify that even before they ask." She gave an example of a unit on the novel *Lord of the Flies* in which they spent a lot of time talking about the "human potential for evil," which she felt was a very relevant topic for them given some of their current questions about difficult things happening in the world. "I'm still working on that, how to change the curriculum based on the emotional needs kids have. I have to make sure I look out for the kids." She reflected, "I am much more understanding of what works and what doesn't; I am more conscious of kids with different needs and different learning styles."

Through refining her understanding of her subject in greater relationship to her students, Andrea was beginning to develop pedagogical content knowledge (Shulman, 1986, 1987). As Shulman and his colleagues have explained, the relationship between content and learners is central to the special kind of knowledge teachers need:

> Successful teachers cannot simply have an intuitive or personal understanding of a particular concept, principle or theory. Rather, in order to foster understanding, they must themselves understand ways of *representing* the concept for students. They must have knowledge of the ways of transforming the concept for students. They must have knowledge of the ways of transforming the content for the purposes of teaching. In Dewey's terms, they must "psychologize" the subject matter. In order to transform or psychologize the subject matter, teachers must have a knowledge of the subject matter that includes a personal understanding of the content as well as knowledge of ways to communicate that understanding, to foster the development of subject matter knowledge in the minds of students. (Wilson, Shulman, & Richert, 1987, p. 110)

Andrea noted that an understanding of children's personal needs, the context of their lives and how it shaped their learning, and her appreciation for making curriculum relevant to them was a new and emerging understanding for her. While teaching at Jefferson, she did not often get to know her students personally: "It was too draining." She reflected that looking back, she feels foolish that she was unable to do so, but adds that at the time, "I was not sure I could deal with it."

ILLUSIONS DASHED OR VISION MAINTAINED?

In some ways, Andrea tells a familiar story. An inexperienced, new teacher is placed in the challenging circumstance of teaching children different from herself (having had little coaching or mentoring to help her approach that situation) in a school with little collegial support and with few resources. In the end, she chooses to leave the students she cares about and elects to leave the public school she had hoped to make a difference in. In some ways, though, this story departs from the expected ending of that narrative. Andrea does not leave teaching. In fact, over time, through bringing her understanding and insights about students into balance with her passion for her subject matter by making clearer her dreams for what students might achieve through literature, Andrea feels that she has deepened and solidified her commitment to her teaching. She feels closer to her dreams about what she could achieve, and attributes that progress to learning about her students—about their needs, strengths, and capabilities. Thus, in an interview 4 years after that conversation and while still teaching at St. Mark's,[2] Andrea felt more certain than ever that teaching is the right profession for her now.

Yet the story is of course not so simple. Andrea felt responsible for what she and her Jefferson students could not accomplish—sometimes locating the problem with herself, sometimes the community, sometimes her students. She seriously considered leaving teaching after her very first year teaching full-time. Even more worrisome, her experience of the gap between vision and reality led Andrea to question her initial belief that all students can learn. Furthermore, the nagging issues with which she left Jefferson, concerns that children in that low-income community might not have the capacity to accomplish what she had hoped for them, were not ones that she has had much of a chance to revisit. And while she is now having more positive experiences, she has not left those experiences behind. Her experience leaves important questions about her expectations and what she learned about children. Did Andrea, as Sarah so eloquently described in Chapter 1, "give up" her "illusions"—did she water down her vision for students at Jefferson so much that it no longer reflected her high expectations? Or did she actually maintain her vision by adjusting it in realistic and appropriate ways? Indeed, what would it have taken for her to accomplish it, to "overcome the obstacles"? Andrea's experiences raise a wealth of questions of interest to those who want to support the growth, development, and commitment of new inspired teachers like her, and help them conclude that their dreams *are* possible.

Teaching Through the Wormhole

It was a cold Sunday morning in February 1998. I reached for the telephone to call Kelly, to find out how her school year was going. After 5 years of teaching science at Blackwell, a large suburban public high school in an upper-middle-class community in California, she had moved across the country to Hilltop High School, a newly established, small, urban alternative school in a low-income community in Massachusetts. Hilltop had begun as a pilot program in a large public high school and had been a separate school for only 3 years. The move involved many changes for Kelly: From working in a school with a staff of roughly 90, she was now going to be one of 9 full-time teachers; from working in a shared classroom with a team of science and math teachers, she would now be the sole science teacher in her classroom; from teaching students from largely middle- and upper-middle-class families (Blackwell's population had been 53% White, 29% Asian, 11% Latino/a, 4% African American, and 3% other), she would now be working with a group of students from mostly low-income families (Hilltop's student population was 65% African American, 25% Latino, 5% Vietnamese, and 5% White).

The previous time I had spoken with Kelly, she was still at Blackwell and was finishing her last year there. She had said she had been pleased with her accomplishments as a teacher and with the successes of her Blackwell students, but did not feel that she had yet been able to fully enact her vision of students as independent scientific thinkers. In fact, at that time she felt that her vision lay at quite a significant distance from her current practice.

But when I called her 6 months into her first year at Hilltop, things seemed completely different. Her perception of the distance between her vision and her practice had changed quite significantly. In fact, she explained that this year felt worlds apart from all her previous years in teaching. She and her Hilltop colleagues might actually be able to accomplish her vision. She mused, "It's like the first time I think we have staff . . . where everybody is not only open to it but we're actually going to try it. We're actually going to try and implement it." She described a mixture of eagerness, hope, and anxiety that accompanies that realization.

> I'm nervous because I don't know if it's going to work. I mean I should say if anything I'm very much, I'm very hopeful. I'm very excited because...I don't think I've ever been this close to making this vision come true. To being part of making the vision come true. . . . And so I'm, you know, it's one of those things where—what do you call it? It's like, we're going to walk the walk essentially, and I'm scared.

While Kelly was extremely happy about her new school and the possibilities for reaching her vision, her new school was in a new state, which had recently initiated a new set of standardized tests, tests that could have an enormous impact on the future of her teaching, her students' success, and her school. The Massachusetts Comprehensive Assessment System (MCAS) tests were to be piloted in her district for several years, and then would take effect for the graduating class of 2004. At that time, students would not be able to graduate high school if they were unable to pass the tests. The new testing context weighed heavily on Kelly. Thus, while Kelly attributed her anxiety to her own responsibility, she also explained that at times her fears evolved into questioning whether the vision she and her colleagues had developed was ultimately one that would benefit the students. She posed a string of concerns,

> It's more . . . [like] will I be able to carry out my role? And what's going to happen? Is this good? Is this in the end good for the students? Or are we going to take them on this trip . . . where we don't know where it's going to end?

In teaching today, particularly in an era of increased attention to standardized testing, a complex relationship exists between maintaining one's ideals and addressing the demands of accountability. Kelly's experience reveals the relationship between *vision* and *context*: the struggles teachers go through in attempting to balance their dreams with the demands of the broader educational environment. While Andrea (in Chapter 2) focused intently upon her classroom, Kelly's vision had a broader range that spanned her practices in her own classroom as well as the practices of her colleagues and the school organization. Yet just as Andrea began to struggle with the broader context of her school and students, Kelly began to struggle with the broader context of the state. At Blackwell, Kelly had been able to pursue her vision of students engaging in scientific inquiry and independent thinking with little external pressure (other than the not-unimportant concern that her Blackwell students be successful on the Scholastic Aptitude Tests (SAT), and they usually were).[1] So up until this year Kelly had been able to "stick to her guns" and make sure that she continued her efforts to get closer to her vision.

However, one of the reasons Kelly moved to Hilltop was that she hoped to get closer to the ideal classroom practice she had dreamed about while still at Blackwell. But at Hilltop, she was suddenly teaching a student population for whom she felt the stakes were much higher, and the success much more uncertain. She had to face the fact that her students would endure 2 solid weeks of the high-stakes MCAS examinations, tests that emphasized discrete facts and rote recall of scientific terms and processes—an emphasis she felt was at odds with her vision (and Hilltop's vision) of students as self-sufficient thinkers and intrinsically motivated learners.

So while research has demonstrated that the classroom practices of many teachers are shaped by school and departmental contexts (e.g., McLaughlin & Talbert, 1993), Kelly's experience demonstrates how the state and national context can play a significant role in teaching as well. In particular, her experience demonstrates what happens when a teacher's vision is at odds with the state context. While Kelly holds extremely high standards for herself and her students, which are rooted in her vision of good teaching, her conception is quite different from that embodied by the state standards. Such dramatic opposition poses challenges to her confidence about her teaching and to her vision for her students. In fact, some recent research on teachers' responses to state- and district-level policies has focused upon how they make sense of these mandates, examining how teachers interpret, manage, and negotiate the meanings of different reform initiatives (e.g., Coburn, 2001; Spillane, Reiser, & Reimer, 2002). Yet it seems that for Kelly, the state policies do not prompt as benign a response as sense making. The state policies intrude upon practice and lead her to unsettling concerns, fears, and doubts. The dramatic opposition between her vision and that of the state leads her to questions about her vision, the abilities of her students, as well as her own ability to teach.

At the same time, some current examinations of classroom teaching in light of standardized testing suggest that often teachers quite dramatically change their practice in response to statewide testing. These studies reveal that teachers tend to give more attention to the content of the tests in their daily lessons (McMillan, Myran, & Workman, 1999) and that teachers are also deemphasizing content not on the test (Jones et al., 1999; Koretz, Barron, Mitchell, & Steecher, 1996). Abrams, Pedulla, and Madaus (2003), who surveyed over four thousand teachers from what they termed "high-stakes" and "low-stakes" states, found that a substantial number of teachers in both testing programs reported that their statewide tests had led them to teach in ways that run counter to their own beliefs about good educational practices.

Yet this story of Kelly's experience is not quite as simple. It does not detail how she had to give up her ideals due to the demands of accountability and standardization. Nor is it a straightforward story of her resistance to such pressures. Rather, this is the story of the ways in which this externally imposed context of accountability shakes her confidence, shifts her curriculum, and shapes her learning about her teaching, her students, and her school. And it is also the story of how, due to the clarity of her vision and the compatible fit between her vision and her school context, she stays the course.

Kelly's experience also shows that a teacher's ability to resolve that tension depends upon the relationship between subject matter and students in one's vision. Andrea's story illustrated that developing an understanding of her students and their world in a deeper way—developing her vision of them—vastly contributed to her feelings of success and efficacy. She had had a clear vision of subject but not of students, and once she brought the two into greater balance, she began to feel more productive and effective as a teacher. Kelly gives us a glimpse of a more experienced teacher, at a later stage in her career. While Andrea had yet to bring subject matter and students into balance, at this point in Kelly's career her vision reflected both a balanced view of subjects and of students. For instance, while at Blackwell, she had focused upon how to help students have a voice in the development of curriculum. Yet by the time she was in her third year at Hilltop, she was thinking about how best to foster students' development of concepts, which concepts to focus upon, and how to design curriculum that was not only relevant to students but also able to gradually build their understanding of specific ideas, approaches, and ways of thinking—all within the context of high-pressure testing. Indeed, Kelly's experience demonstrates how a deep relationship between students and subject can feed one another, strengthening one's teaching vision. In turn, that vision enables a teacher like Kelly to make informed decisions about how to best negotiate her various contexts—not only those that support her vision but those that seem in conflict with it.

KELLY'S VISION

When describing her vision in a written statement while a fifth-year teacher at Blackwell High School, Kelly does not talk about the physical layout of the classroom, but rather portrays the atmosphere of the classroom. Her vision is one in which students and teacher explore scientific questions together in an atmosphere of "excitement, earnestness, and life." Investigations are shaped by student interest rather than by teacher's choice or textbook topics. The environment is charged with excitement; Kelly sees herself "surrounded" by students who have questions "burgeoning" from them, and she sees herself responding with "guidance, coaching, and shared enthusiasm." She also imagines students asking one another the same questions "with the same demand and expectation they ask of me, as though they knew the question was their own, not mine, thus making the answer more important to discover." Students are learning to question and challenge information they've encountered and are learning to think critically through real-world problems: They "investigate and offer solutions to complex situations which often have no answer, while developing skills and reflecting on their learning." Kelly imagines students working in a variety of different forms determined by what is appropriate to the task at hand: "some in groups, some individually, in discussions and research working on problems that are real-world, practical."

Kelly describes her role in this classroom as "resource provider," which she contrasts to "knowledge provider." She explains:

> I feel this is important to remove myself from the role of "information center" and "curriculum dictator" because too often the teacher becomes a human answer key, to whom students go to check their solutions. Teachers should be guides so as to encourage the students to pursue something of an intrinsic motivation. Teacher-centered classes motivate students extrinsically, by steering the class in one direction, one interest.

An important aspect of Kelly's role is also acting as the human representative of her subject matter. While Kelly recognizes that one could interpret this notion as "a very teacher-centered role," she explains that one could also think about it quite differently. She sees her role as the facilitator of the kind of "two-way road" that she hopes students will enjoy in her classroom between their own interests and that of the discipline of science.

While Kelly's vision focuses upon students becoming independent thinkers, able to approach problems with confidence and thoughtfulness, her vision has more than one focal point, it moves beyond her classroom. Kelly envisions a school in which colleagues also have those goals for students. Teachers who share the vision could reinforce the kind of approach Kelly takes in her classroom by offering similar approaches to teaching and learning in their own classrooms. Thus the students would have a consistent experience across classes. Without that consistency Kelly believes that her students would get mixed messages about learning:

> They [would] leave my class and go somewhere else, and I don't know where they go. I don't know if their next period is going to be with a teacher who believes only in lectures, or with a teacher who isn't emphasizing those skills.

In addition, Kelly adds, such consistent approaches would enable students to sustain their independent learning because they would encounter it in all their classes, not simply hers. She feels that a shared, schoolwide approach would be more likely to contribute to attitudes and approaches to lifelong learning. "[Otherwise] they may learn something [just] in my class. But I would like them to develop a lifelong habit."

Kelly emphasizes that an extremely important part of her vision was ongoing, strong relationships with such like-minded colleagues. She likens her image of herself in her vision to an "octopus, with all these tentacles" suggesting that as a teacher she imagines having a "huge network" of lines of communication to colleagues. Thus she could support her students with the assistance of fellow teachers and staff who would know the students equally well and could contribute their perspectives of the students from other arenas in different subjects and classes. Indeed, the broad range of Kelly's vision reflects her insistence and understanding that such collegial (and institutional) supports are necessary to enact her classroom vision: "I feel like the collegiality makes this structure [of my vision] possible, more effective, than if I were doing this by myself. In fact, I don't think I could do this by myself." Kelly also explains that such collegiality would also enable her to put the time and thought into the sort of classroom she wants to create; it would allow her to have a more flexible schedule and would support her own professional development and reflection.

> On a curricular level, the collegiality makes the education a lot richer. [It] makes, for instance, the flexible use of time possible, that [we] would need in order to give [us] the time to actually sit together and be working on these projects in groups; to set up small seminars where [we] talk about things or reflect about what just happened.

Finally, Kelly also imagines that her school would ideally be connected to the community in such a way that students' coursework could be based in part upon current problems or issues being addressed by that community. As she explains in her vision statement, "I . . . see much community involvement—projects that reach into the society they live in, as well as the active participation of community members in the classroom. Schools should act as conduits between society and students."

School is a society; students are in society, but with different concerns than the greater society.

"STILL VERY FAR AWAY": THE YEARS AT BLACKWELL

The first time I spoke with Kelly, in June 1997, she explained that though she and her Blackwell High colleagues had made some progress, her vision lay at a significant distance from her current practice. In particular, despite the fact that Kelly and her colleagues (who were team-teaching in an alternative school within a school called the Academy program at Blackwell) attempted to provide consistent messages about learning across all classes, the students still did not approach learning in the ways that they hoped they would. She worried, "We're still very far away, I think, from students really owning their education." Kelly felt that Academy students at Blackwell had a tendency to be invested in their education for extrinsic reasons such as obtaining good grades toward admittance into a prestigious college, rather than for the excitement of learning itself. She related one incident that occurred just before our initial interview that illustrated her students' focus on grades.

> In one of my classes [in] the conversation toward the end, an issue opened up about whether you do things because you want to do them or you do things because of grades. And the students, at one point some of these students (who I think very much respect me as a teacher, and we have a close rapport) were very honest and said, "Let's just face it . . . you care too much; we don't even care at all. We would rather just have you tell us what to do because we need the As to get into college."

Kelly added that though she and her colleagues had been "successful" in helping Blackwell Academy students identify and explore topics of personal interest, she still found that her students emphasized their grades and not their development as learners:

> They'll still get their grades back, and [ask], "Why did *you* give me an A?" As opposed to them turning it in and saying, "This is definitely a work in progress," or "This is a culminating work for me." They just don't have any sort of reflectiveness about that.

Kelly noticed that the students in the Academy program tended to compare their program to that of students in the traditional program. And rather than understanding that they were learning powerful approaches to information, she felt the Academy students were focusing upon the content knowledge that they were "missing." *Not fully developed cognitively?*

> I think there's a lot of stress for students comparing themselves to the other students . . . in the traditional program. More often then not, they'll say, "We're behind," because we haven't covered something that somebody else [has], rather than seeing what they're learning as being advanced. For instance, we were covering basic trigonometry in November of this year in geometry, whereas all geometry students in

the traditional [program] never get there until the end of the year. But that didn't register in my students' heads as "This is advanced." They just thought, "Why aren't we learning proofs? Why aren't we learning what the other kids are learning?"

In order to get closer to their vision, Kelly felt that she and her Blackwell colleagues needed to help the Academy students rethink the purposes of school. She mused, "It's almost like reshaping what their perception of what school is." Kelly also reflected that though her colleagues appeared to agree on a school vision, differences arose around the means of achieving the vision.

Two years ago, I remember having these staff meetings about our vision as a school. And it seemed like most people agreed to the same sort of tenets about structuring education for the students. But it seemed like we could never quite agree on how to get there. . . . When we begin proposing pathways of how to get there . . . there definitely is this tension about which pathway is the best to go, and that one pathway threatens another pathway. So that's . . . where we get stuck.

Kelly looked forward to her new school, Hilltop, where all teachers—and all students—shared the same focus and goals. In fact, Kelly noted that she had reread her written description of her vision the day before her interview at Hilltop, as a way to revisit again in very concrete ways what her goals and dreams were for her teaching. She felt strongly that one of the reasons she had chosen to work at Hilltop was its consistency with her vision.

SO CLOSE AND YET SO FAR: THE MOVE TO HILLTOP

So Close

The following winter (1998) at her new school, Hilltop High School, Kelly described anticipating that her vision was imminent. She felt that she and her colleagues were actually going to attempt to implement her—and their—vision. Kelly and her colleagues were creating a plan to support the development of independent thinking in students that involved focusing on different levels of thinking for students. They had identified what they called an Inquiry Level for younger students to learn how to approach problems, pose good questions, and reflect on their work (essentially, learn metacognitive skills). Then they had identified a Self-Initiating Level at which students would be able to identify areas of interest to them and pursue them somewhat independently. Kelly felt that she and her colleagues at Hilltop were beginning to make very concrete what she had imagined in her vision.

And, in fact, one of her classes that spring, in which her students take a trip to the Boston Public Library to conduct research for group projects, helps illustrate the growing consistency between her vision and her practice as well as some of the challenges with which Kelly continues to wrestle. In particular, the class demonstrates the ways in which Kelly seems to have been able to put the following elements of her vision into practice:

- Her focus upon independent student learning (her students were investigating and reporting on diseases such as AIDS, breast cancer, and sickle cell anemia)
- Her role as a facilitator and coach
- Her emphasis upon knowing students well (her students began each class telling stories about their weekend and also reflecting upon their learning)
- Her vision of relationships with colleagues (several of her fellow teachers accompanied her on the library trip, which she says is part of the school ethos and for her, made the trip possible)

A PICTURE OF PRACTICE: STUDENTS' INDEPENDENT RESEARCH PROJECTS

Hilltop High School sits at the top of a little hill in a city outside Boston, past neatly kept gray and brown wooden and brick duplexes clustered close together. It is a grand, elegant square building with an iron fence outside that has the façade of a government building or a bank. In Kelly's classroom, there are six tables with chairs around them and another table at the front of the room with a computer on it. Student work is displayed on the walls, as well as a few posters and several sheets on which Kelly had written some classroom norms, rules, and suggestions. On the back wall was a sheet with the question, "What's in a reflection?" followed by a number of phrases:

- *A statement of where you are in terms of your learning.*
- *"Before" and "After" case.* "In the beginning of the trimester...Now, I understand . . . "
- *Refer to the Habits of Lifelong Learning.* "This assignment is connected to. . . . It's related to . . . This has helped me see from a different perspective . . . "
- *Honest about what you know/don't know.* "Even though I understand this and this, I still have problems with . . . "

The period begins with what Kelly calls Reflections, in which the ninth graders share "stories," which are mostly recounts of their weekends, and "connections," in which students share goals for the day or week (students talk about doing well on particular tests, doing better in particular subjects). Her student Takesha facilitates this session, which involves inviting students to participate and also telling some students not to interrupt others.

After Reflections, Kelly explains what the class will be doing today. She reminds the students that they are going to go to the library for the next 2 hours. She wants every group to locate at least one, and up to three or four, articles and between two and four books on their topic. She asks them to fill out a worksheet detailing the name, title, year, and some notes from each source they obtained.

Her class sets off for the library with backpacks, notebooks, and subway passes organized. Two full-time teachers accompany them, as well as a student teacher. Kelly explains that the whole "cluster" of students were going—all of the ninth graders. Once at the library, Kelly quickly checks in with some of the students who want to ask a quick question, while most of the students head off to various areas in the library to begin researching.

Kelly spends the rest of the morning moving from group to group in the library, helping students or groups with computer or Internet searches, or with other questions. At one point, Kelly and one of the other full-time teachers, Carolyn, sit down together at a table, taking a break from their patrolling. They marvel together at "how far" the students had come in terms of what they could do now. Kelly comments that the students seemed to be getting better at organizing their time during a 2-hour block.

After class, Kelly talked more about her reactions to the library trip: "I think today I felt mildly surprised that most of the kids were working. . . . It's really made me understand . . . how far they have come." She noted that she had worried a little bit the night before about the independent nature of the work at the library—would they know how to use their time? Had she prepared them well enough to find useful and appropriate resources? She could tell that some of the students had not remembered that they had planned to go, but she was still happy that they had been able to "do fairly well" in their research. "I'm happy overall . . . with what I saw today," she concluded.

Indeed, Kelly felt that this particular day shared some aspects that are consistent with her vision:

> I . . . was envisioning them being relatively independent learners where they're working more or less independently and I would act more as a coach. And . . . surprisingly, I think today kind of fit that a little more than I had done in the past. It seemed like today a lot of it was maneuvering around and helping kids. . . . I was able to go around and act more as a coach than . . . [as] the sole dispenser of knowledge type of thing.

The stability and clarity of her vision was apparent in these reflections: She noted that she felt like she was able to facilitate and coach—rather than be the source of knowledge—a key part of her vision.

Kelly did anticipate some difficulties the following day, when the students would need to read their resources and begin to make sense of them for their reports.

> The key is going to be [tomorrow]. I'm worried about tomorrow and Wednesday, trying to [continue my coach role]. I think I'm going to have to fight that a lot, actually, for kids not to pull me down and say, "Tell me what this book says" or "Tell me what this article says." So that'll be interesting!

This glimpse of her classroom also provides an example of the role a strong vision may play in supporting thoughtful and balanced "of the moment" evaluations of students' progress. While Kelly noted that she had felt generally pleased with their degree of independence, she recognized a few supports she might provide next time that would make students' work go even more smoothly (going over a map of the library; providing a sheet with some questions that might guide their research). Having a vision allowed her to quickly evaluate their work in light of it, and enabled her to also identify some strategies she might use the next time around in order to help her and them do even better work together.

And Yet So Far: Worrying About Wormholes

Yet even though Kelly was in a school that helped her support the kind of independent student work and project-based curriculum that was consistent with her vision, Kelly was still concerned, even fearful. For just 6 months into her first year at Hilltop, it had become very clear that she was in a different state. While Kelly was pleased with the thoughtful, integrated inquiry-based curriculum she had developed with her Hilltop colleagues, she was uneasy about her students' potential performance on the MCAS tests. This concern weighed heavily on Kelly, even though she felt confident that her vision (and that of the school) really represented what was effective for students.

While she expressed hope, Kelly did not offer metaphors consistent with that hope, such as nirvana, Eden, or heaven. Rather, she talked about "wormholes." So while in some ways she felt closer, she had developed new concerns and fears about her vision and her efficacy in enacting it. And at times she even wondered whether the vision she and her colleagues had developed was one that would benefit the students: "You know what it is? . . . This is very geeky, but in *Star Trek* there's this concept of the wormhole, right?" She elaborated:

You jump in one end and you end up on the other side of the universe, right? There was this one episode one time that showed a wormhole where one end point was stable but the other end point wasn't. And so they couldn't sell the rights to go travel this wormhole because you wouldn't know where you would end up. And that's what I feel like. It's like we have just identified the wormhole . . . and we're about to jump into it and I have no idea. I hope that the end point is where the vision is going to be. I'm scared that we're going to take our students on this trip and we may end up in some place completely different.

In fact, it seemed that the conditions were right for meeting her vision but that a very real and particularly unsettling possibility had emerged. What if Kelly and her colleagues teach in a way that is consistent with the vision, but the students do *not* achieve in a way that Kelly envisions, or worse, in a way that they need in order to progress to the next step in their education? Indeed, while the stakes for Kelly were high—with the potential for failure as a teacher—she recognized, and feared, that the stakes for her students even higher. While failure for her would be depressing and dispiriting, for her students it could alter or even suppress opportunities for lifetime success. Perhaps the journey would conclude in a location that constrains her students from making additional, exciting forays to higher education or other arenas for learning and growth.

Shifting Her Curriculum

By late spring Kelly's concerns about subject matter knowledge had mounted. The Hilltop students were right in the midst of taking the MCAS tests that were being piloted in her district along with some others in the city. Though she identified many "flaws" in the tests, Kelly appreciated that a poor performance could have a dramatic impact on her students' futures. She explained that such tests were forcing her to rethink the means to her vision and to focus more upon the content of science rather than the process:

In terms of my concerns, I've been actually very concerned about substance. And it's leading me to sort of rethink a little bit. . . . Not so much that I question the sort of relevance and perspective and even thematic units, but I sense even more so, I guess, the urgency that . . . in order for these students to go on to college and compete on as equal a playing ground as can possibly be, we have to . . . look at content a lot more closely than I ever have before.

Kelly worried that recent critiques of reforming schools might apply to her own students: "Much of the criticism I've heard of reform[ing] schools like Hilltop is that when they get to college [people say that] 'These students are very good in thinking, they're very good in group work, but they are missing the content' and so that handicaps them."

These concerns led Kelly to more questions about the appropriateness of her vision. Sometimes, she said, she worried that she was projecting her own wishes and desires upon her students. Perhaps her vision reflected the educational experiences she herself would have loved to experience, but perhaps not those that were appropriate for her students. She remarked,

> This is the kind of classroom I would enjoy right now. . . . [But] is that vision the kind of classroom they see themselves [as] being the best bet? Maybe my manifestation is different than what these students...maybe it's too limiting for these students. Maybe I should be thinking of more things, more ways that they would—or I should say different scenarios in which they would—become actualized learners.

Yet at the same time, Kelly chose not to dramatically alter her curriculum in light of the tests. She remained faithful to her vision of powerful educational experiences for her students by seeking an appropriate balance between state-required content and process in her curriculum that would still allow her to remain faithful to her vision:

> My vision is not altered . . . I don't think I'm going to spend more time lecturing and memorizing and giving tests or anything like that. I don't envision it like that. I still envision . . . finding ways to do labs, to do projects to help build that into their understanding. So I think my vision is . . . not altered, it's just perhaps I need to be more precise in structuring my class.

Kelly revised her curriculum to enable her students to learn more of the content of the tests, but she felt strongly that she would not "alter" her vision. In the face of this pressure cooker of personal, collegial, school, state, and even national stakes, Kelly and her colleagues displayed remarkable courage and faith. They pursued their vision, hopeful that they were doing the right thing. They tried to reasonably adjust their efforts to account for their concerns.

STAYING THE COURSE: THIRD AND FOURTH YEARS AT HILLTOP

"I Felt Closer Than Ever"

By Kelly's third and fourth years at Hilltop, she had begun to enjoy some more feelings of success, though not without underlying questions and doubts. When I interviewed her after her third year, in the summer of 2000, she noted,

"This year, I felt closer than ever. I really feel optimistic." Kelly felt that she had developed some curriculum that really reflected her vision's emphasis upon independent thinking. She noted that she had "come a lot closer to the vision." For example, she explained that she had developed a project in which students investigated the quality of water in their city. The project was intended to help her students understand the relevance of science to their community, hone their inquiry skills, practice independent investigation, and develop more experience in quantitative science. Over the course of several months, students collected samples of water from their homes, school, and community centers; ran tests; graphed results; analyzed the data; and wrote reports. Kelly had received a grant for the unit, through which she had cultivated a connection with a highly respected local university and with the Environmental Protection Agency, which offered to conduct lead tests on the water samples for free (normally they were very expensive). Both organizations were particularly eager to help out because they also wanted to make use of the data gathered by her students.

In the middle of their research, students presented their findings to a set of teachers and reformers at a national conference sponsored by the Coalition of Essential Schools. And, at the end of their investigation, students presented the findings to an audience of parents, teachers, and other community members. In many ways, Kelly said she felt convinced about the quality and nature of their learning, and was extremely pleased with the passion and engagement they had displayed over the course of the project. She was also excited about the way she had been able to connect their work with the other organizations. In that way, her students could see the very real impact and import of their research.

At the same time, Kelly was not entirely satisfied with the work she and her students had done; she continued to push her own expectations and those she held of her students. While Kelly felt thrilled in some ways with their progress, she still believed that in some ways the students' work was not quite of the quality she envisioned. She pointed out areas where she and they could improve their work even more. In particular, she felt she might need to do a better job helping them develop their presentation skills in order to share scientific data with an audience. Kelly explained that when her students had trouble meeting her expectations, she "tended to look at [her] teaching" rather than feel that her vision was not appropriate for them. She continued to examine her practice in light of those ideals, constantly identifying ways in which she and her students can improve their work.

Building a Bridge

Kelly felt that much of this accomplishment in designing experiences like the water quality project came from understanding her students better. She explained that she was beginning to envision teaching as "building a bridge" between her vision and her students. She noted that the original image of the "two-way road" between her subject and her students had really captured something important about teaching for her. Yet she reflected that over the past few years as a teacher, she felt she had been concentrating more upon her subject—upon the concepts and ideas in science she wanted them to understand—rather than upon who her students were.

But over the past couple of years at Hilltop, she felt that she had gained a much better sense of who her students were, what they needed, and what they were able to do. She recalled that when she first started at Hilltop, she had "assumed a certain level of understanding and skill"—for instance, assuming that her students could divide and multiply well in order to perform some of the necessary calculations in her class. However, she had really needed to "relearn and reevaluate" her understanding of her students, identifying areas of improvement and strength. By her second year at Hilltop, her understanding of her students was "more solidly grounded," and she felt she had a much better appreciation for "how to foster [their] concept development." In this way, she felt she was gradually able to "inject a lot more independent learning" that she envisioned, and build student confidence, as well as her own.

What Kelly's experience suggests is that as a teacher learns about her students and as she concurrently learns more about her subject, the two begin to "feed" one another, helping provide an even more solid foundation for a teacher's vision. In turn, refining one's vision of subject and students ultimately helps shape appropriate teaching strategies and curriculum that function well both in terms of subject and students. In essence, Kelly was getting better and better at creating what Bruner (1960/1977) terms "intellectually honest" curriculum, curriculum that teaches the essential concepts in one's discipline while recognizing what is appropriate and generative for students' cognitive and emotional level. Kelly reflected that she was now both "concentrating upon content" and also constantly tuning that vision of content to her vision of her students. Rather than a two-way road, she now said, "I'm building a bridge from both sides."

But her work with her students within her school was also taking place within a state context that continued to threaten the stability of that bridge. When asked about the MCAS tests, Kelly said, "It's very difficult. . . . We tend to treat it as if we are doing the best we can." Having scrutinized the test, she noted that it still focused upon "random concepts" that ran in complete contradiction to the ways in which she was trying to help her students appreciate the field of science.[2] Despite the fact that Kelly was engaging her students in what seemed to be a quite sophisticated rendering of a scientific experience—identifying a problem that was authentic in their community concerning the nature of their water, gathering data, developing hypotheses, evaluating the data, testing hypotheses, representing the data through graphs and other visuals, and finally sharing the data with a real audience and answering unanticipated questions from that audience—the test the students were required to take did not reflect *any* of that scientific understanding. Unfortunately, over the past 3 years (and like other students in the city district), her students had done quite poorly on the pilot exams.[3] And, Kelly added, the stakes were even higher because her ninth graders (who would graduate in 2004) now had to pass the test to advance to the tenth grade. Thus, at the same time, Kelly felt increasing tension between the accomplishment of her students and what the state was expecting—between the fact that she was working toward her vision *and* making sure her students enjoyed success on the tests. The academic year 2000-2001 was also the first time that the tests would have very real and extremely consequential impacts on her students' futures since previous years had been pilot years.[4]

However, Kelly was able to acknowledge the importance of the tests but still maintain the confidence that "we are doing the best we can." She remained certain that her students were developing powerful scientific understandings in her courses, and she was able to conclude that while she would try to address some of the content knowledge assessed by the tests, "I'm not going to teach to [the tests]." She was able to say with some assurance, "I know what we are teaching them is strong." She also acknowledged that it is "very important" to work on her students' skills and emphasized, "I recognize—am aware—that at least for this population I teach, I have to make sure that they have the skills *down*."

OF ROADS, WORMHOLES, AND BRIDGES

Figuring out how to hold on to one's ideals while confronting the realities of the classroom is of special importance in this era of increased accountability. For teachers who find their vision at odds with their context, this disconnect may be particularly difficult. For Kelly, the demands of the Massachusetts standardized tests stand in sharp contrast to the practice she envisions. However, having a clear sense of purpose rooted in her strong, well-articulated professional vision helps Kelly stick to her principles, even in the face of significant state pressure. In particular, the clarity of her vision helps Kelly assess her students' progress in her classroom, on particular projects, and on the tests. She can compare their work to what she hopes they will—and thinks they can—accomplish, and can make judgments about their development. Being able to evaluate her students' development in this way also helps her put the tests into perspective, enabling her to question them appropriately while still appreciating the important role they will likely play in her students' lives.

Kelly's growing understanding of how to negotiate the relationship between her ideals and the reality of the classroom may also contribute to her feelings of confidence. She had the luxury of learning how to manage this potential gap for several years in a school that did not emphasize test performance as much, during a time that the state of California had also not yet "upped the ante" with regard to standardized testing. Had she started her work in Massachusetts, she might not have had the opportunity to articulate her vision and imagine the steps to reach it, which in fact may have been crucial for her development.

A second element of Kelly's feelings of success may be found in the bridge she described between her students and her subject. She found that working toward what she wanted her students to accomplish in science happened most powerfully when she began to understand and appreciate her students even more as learners. Andrea's story in Chapter 2 called attention to the importance of bringing an understanding of one's students into balance with an understanding of one's subject. Kelly's experience further develops that point, demonstrating how the balance between subject and students actually "feed" one another in vision. The more Kelly thought about the key concepts she felt her students should be learning, the more she found she needed to think about *how* students might learn the subject matter and in what ways she might connect it to their own lives and interests. In turn, the more she understood about her students (how children developed an understanding of science, what interested them about the subject, how to connect it to their own experiences), the more she learned about her own understanding of science (what were the key ideas in science, what were foundational scientific methods and modes of inquiry; what types of investigations might call upon those kinds of knowledge). Indeed, through thinking about her vision, Kelly was gradually developing, refining, and elaborating her pedagogical content knowledge (Shulman, 1986, 1987; Wilson et al., 1987)—knowledge that Andrea also developed through thinking about her vision, her subject, and her students. For this experience, it may have been important for Kelly to move to a new school context, in which she faced challenges brought by a new population of children with whom she was not accustomed to work. She had to, as she put it, "relearn" about her students, developing a greater understanding of their strengths, needs, and areas for improvement that in turn initiated a deeper exploration of her content.

Ultimately, Kelly's ability to manage the tension between her vision for her classroom and school and the demands of the state came about as she negotiated a reasonable balance between the needs of teaching challenging content with the needs and interests of her students. By identifying what her students most needed to learn in science, and by deepening her understanding of how to foster understanding in her students, she was able to remain clear about her priorities (and theirs) and to make a reasonable attempt to address some of the material on the exams, while not focusing solely upon the content covered by the exams. Indeed, she was able to maintain her sense of purpose, making sure it seemed as appropriate as possible for her students' needs and goals, and was able also to try to attend to the development of their skills, which will be assessed by the exams.

In fact, an examination of the images Kelly used to describe her vision and elements of her vision call attention to the development of her thinking—from a two-way road, to a wormhole, to a bridge. Her first metaphor describing subjects and students was the two-way road, indicating how her students could have input into the curriculum. While a two-way road has a clear destination and takes into account both subject and students, it also leaves open the possibility of "passing in the night" without making any connection. Further, the path is not necessarily shared—not everyone is traveling in the same direction. And while the later metaphor of the wormhole does suggest a shared path (everyone is traveling together in the same direction), travelers enter at one end and are jettisoned out the other, with no knowledge of the course they traversed to get to the other side. In addition, in a wormhole, travelers have no control over where they end up—they could easily be exited to a place that is not at all desirable. However, the metaphor of bridge building illustrates the advancement in her thinking. The bridge is particularly compelling because it suggests not only a shared path, but also a clear sense of how to get there and careful control over the construction of the path. Furthermore, the notion of building suggests steps built one at a time, controlled by her and her students, gradually making progress in order to share a connection.

Kelly's experience building such bridges has not been easy. Nor has she completely resolved the tension between the testing required by the state with the vision she has for her students' high achievement, self-sufficiency, and deep understanding of science. She continues to navigate the difficult territory of those multiple demands, still wrestling with doubts, questions, and even sometimes fears for her student's futures. Yet she continues to push her expectations for her students, herself, and her school, sustained by her commitment to her vision. As Duffy (1998) has argued, teaching of this nature requires "mental strength, independence, and courage" (p. 780) that comes from the confidence of having vision. For Kelly, her vision provides her with that much-needed faith and courage, fueling her hopes to build bridges for years to come.

Chapter 4

Teaching Toward Powerful Moments

When I first met Jake in June 1997, he had just completed his seventh year of teaching, which was his first year at Parkside High School, a large comprehensive public high school in California's Bay Area. Jake had recently left the traditional high school where he had been teaching social studies for 6 years. He had sought a job at Parkside because he believed that he might be better able to pursue the kinds of teaching he was coming to envision. He knew that Parkside was beginning to explore some curricular reforms modeled after the Coalition of Essential Schools,[1] and he felt that those reforms complemented his ideals about what schooling and teaching should be. Jake felt charged with excitement and energy as he moved into this new job: "Now I know that this school could be a place where some things like [my vision] happen. It's energizing."

But he also noted that he was taking a long view about his progress:

> But you have to step back and realize it's not happening right now, it's probably not going to happen tomorrow, and I'm not going to get too worked up about it. But I think I'm very conscious of *this* as something that could happen . . . it happens enough to know that it's possible. And I definitely have come to the place where I realize things aren't going to change overnight and that you need to be patient with the process. So I guess it's an ongoing process. . . . You see this happening, not all the time, but some of the time. And I think it's possible.

Jake's experiences draw attention to the ways in which vision can drive a teacher's decisions about where to teach, how long to stay, and where to go next. His experiences illustrate how teachers figure out whether there are places that can support their ideals and where they can achieve them. The number of teachers who move from school to school is extremely high. In fact, the phenomenon of teacher mobility, what educational researcher Richard Ingersoll (2001) terms "migration," accounts for about half of the total turnover of teachers in the United States every year. Ingersoll found that teachers who move cite reasons such as a lack of administrative support, low salaries, student discipline problems, or few opportunities to be part of decision making. Others who study the same issues emphasize the influence that rewards and incentives can play in teachers' decisions to stay or leave (Grissmer & Kirby, 1997). Yet recent research on the next generation of teachers—and those new teachers who stay, leave, or move—suggests that of all the factors involved in those decisions, the most salient factor is whether teachers feel successful in teaching (Johnson & Birkeland, 2002).

For teachers like Jake, Kelly, and Andrea, their vision and the match between the vision and their context helps to determine how successful they feel. Over the course of what is now a 15-year career (since we first met), Jake has taught at three different schools, switching two different times. However, Jake did not move to get a better salary, a lighter or less difficult teaching load; in fact, each time his move probably occasioned an equal or more challenging teaching load. Rather, he chose to move to schools that were more consistent with his vision of good teaching and that offered an opportunity to work with colleagues who shared that vision. "Salary wasn't an incentive. These things weren't at the heart of why I wanted to move schools. . . . It was about the opportunity . . . to impact what was happening."

Vision played a role in a range of Jake's decisions, as it did for many other teachers, like Andrea, Kelly, and Carlos. Yet for Jake, vision not only shaped choices about where to teach, how to work with students, and how to design curriculum, but it also influenced his choices about the kinds of learning opportunities and professional development and particular career choices he would make once at a school.

Through these moves, Jake's experiences demonstrate how vision helped maintain his commitment and enthusiasm. Jake used his vision to explicitly make decisions about where to teach: He chose schools that matched his ideal as closely as possible. In between those moves, vision guided him through other decisions about professional development. But throughout, what sustained him was what I call an "episodic" vision. Jake's vision, which focuses upon "moments" of ideal practice as opposed to ideal practice that occurs daily, helps keep him motivated and inspired most of the time. Because Jake does not expect his classroom to reflect his vision all the time but rather to occur in moments that he works up to over time, over weeks and even months of scaffolding, Jake does not lose faith in his vision or in his practice.

JAKE'S VISION

When Jake wrote about what he sees in his ideal classroom as a sixth-year teacher at Parkside High School, he began by talking about different formations of students, all of whom are working together in a variety of ways.

I see students clustered in groups, or working alone, or consulting with me (or another teacher). [I] see a variety of resources that students are consulting—computers, texts, magazines, videos. Students are talking, and asking questions and attempting to solve problems. [They do] not argue or "prove" points but dialogue, discuss, and build solutions. Students are casual, maybe coming in and out of the classroom. Later, students will be presenting their work, answering questions and analyzing their own work and presentations.

Jake's role in his vision is that of a sort of grand marshal of classroom projects. He orchestrates much behind and in front of the classroom scene: formulating problems, gradually scaffolding students' understandings, and urging them toward a completed project or experience. This completed project forms the centerpiece of Jake's vision, what Jake calls "moments." Moments are experiences of deep engagement and significant learning that have lasting influence upon students. A moment occurs when students are reflecting, talking, probing, and deeply engaged in some ideas generated by the course materials. At those times, he observes and supports dialogue, but does not lead discussion or generate questions. As he described it,

what I enjoy most is when I can just sit…there and watch and hear people, hear the students talking in an impassioned voice, in a concerned manner about things that are important in an informed way. Where . . . I'm not telling you [the student], "You have to say this." I might kind of nudge you or—but, those moments when the student who has never thought about government in their life is talking to somebody and really caring about what they think. And they've done the research, they've done enough background to know what they're talking about and having it being meaningful. Those are the moments.

Jake emphasizes that he envisions such moments not only occurring in his own classroom but also happening for all students in his school:

I'm also assuming that this is a schoolwide situation. It's not just me in my classroom—I'm not the only one who's doing this. But I'm working with an English teacher or a science teacher to make these things happen for a certain group of kids.

For instance, the school context should fit well with his emphasis upon designing curriculum and assessing student work. Ideally, he envisions that in this supportive context he is able to focus upon what is important: "I am not worried about paperwork or attendance sheets. I am not preparing for arbitrary standardized tests. I am designing assessments and assessing work, and then discussing student work with the students."

Jake describes his students' ideal roles as "historians and political scientists." They are tireless investigators, rather than those who prove an answer without much hard thinking:

> Students are thinking hard about the job at hand (and are being critical about what they are asked to do). Students are searching for answers as they generate ideas—they search, they don't postulate an answer and then work to prove their assumptions.

Jake imagines that students are learning how to approach, analyze, and understand historical events. "Students learn to use the content as a tool— then study history as a way to answer questions, analyze important problems." Students use a number of different texts—that are "flexible and constantly updated"—from magazines to academic journals to textbooks. Such materials are not seen as the truth, but rather as sources to be critically reviewed, questioned, and used when needed. "Skills" are by no means unimportant; rather, they are to be "integrated" into the teaching. For example, "learn to footnote because your argument would be weaker otherwise." Jake summarizes: "The content changes but the ability to analyze, question, research, communicate, and discuss allows…students to understand [throughout] their whole life."

BEGINNINGS OF VISION: THE YEARS AT FARMINGTON

After graduating from a small university-based teacher education program where he obtained a masters degree in education and a certificate to teach social studies, Jake taught history for 6 years at Farmington High School, a large traditional regional high school in a rural area of northern California. Jake described himself as part of a core cadre of "young hot-shot teachers" who were initiating some reforms at Farmington.

He recalled the experience of planning and implementing new forms of curriculum and assessment as particularly important in his development as a teacher. Yet Jake also noted that even though he and his peers were making some changes, they sometimes faced the frustrating experience that their well-intentioned efforts didn't always end in success: "Even though it was better than what we had done, we were very aware of our failures." He observed, "We had this . . . sense that it wasn't working." He and his colleagues felt that their efforts were not promoting school-wide change, but rather were only working for a subset of children. Jake's perception of the need for change prompted him to critically assess and evaluate his own teaching, curriculum, and school context. It also prompted him to begin to develop a vision of what might be possible. As he put it, "[My] sense that things aren't working . . . has really driven me to think about, 'What *could* we possibly do?'"

Jake eagerly pursued an opportunity to teach at a different school, Parkside High School, that was beginning to make a series of curricular and structural changes that were heavily influenced by the Coalition of Essential Schools such as smaller classes, interdisciplinary coursework, student projects, and alternative assessments. Having carefully researched a number of different opportunities, he sought a job at Parkside. He was offered a position teaching social studies, which he accepted with excitement and anticipation.

VISION FUELS MOTIVATION:
"LET'S JUST CHANGE THE WHOLE THING"

Not surprisingly, Jake quickly jumped into the reform work at Parkside High School during his first year, immediately taking on some leadership roles at the school. He cultivated relationships with colleagues who shared his interest in reform. He remarked with enthusiasm, "I think there are a few teachers who have very similar, not necessarily the exact same vision, but a sense that we [are thinking] let's just change the whole thing. . . . So I think there's that group in our school that's beginning to talk in a serious way." While Jake felt that Parkside had tremendous potential and was certainly making some progress, he also believed that significant distance remained between the current state of the school and what he (and some of his colleagues) envisioned.

Jake had taken the time to observe several days of a formal exhibition of student work at a nearby school, and was very impressed. He felt that such student engagement and self-motivated research fit with what he envisioned his own students doing. Seeing those students present their work gave a kind of concrete possibility to what he had long imagined himself. Spurred by that new understanding about how he could even more fully enact elements of his vision of student engagement, he made a plan to spend time over the summer—without compensation—with his colleagues in order to plan an exhibition project for Parkside senior students. Jake spoke of the enthusiasm he felt when he imagined being able to make some of the elements of his vision concrete, as well as how his vision fueled his determination and commitment:

> I'm really excited about this year, because some time in July some of
> these senior teachers [and I] are going to go off on a hike and camp
> for a night and talk about senior project[s]. So that's the kind of thing
> where it's . . . really exciting. And the Econ teacher and I are going to
> get together and talk about the AP Economics, the AP Government,
> and how we can get the classes to interact and see the connections
> between economics and government. And we're going to do it on our
> own time, not get paid, during the summer. And I guess it's just . . . a
> sacrifice if you want to get anything done.

By the end of the summer, Jake and his colleagues had developed a plan called Senior Exhibitions. The experiences were designed to provide Parkside High School seniors with opportunities to pursue and conduct research on topics of their own interest. (Such projects are typical of Coalition of Essential Schools practice.) Jake and his fellow teachers felt that the seniors would greatly benefit from the experience of pursuing a question of their own, of honing their research and writing skills, and preparing a lengthy written piece. They also saw this plan as an opportunity to engage the community in the assessment of its students. Community members would serve as mentors for projects that interested them or in which they had expertise. They would also serve as an audience, along with fellow students and parents, for the final exhibitions.

Jake explained that he and his colleagues anticipated that the presentation of their projects before an audience would become a "moment" the high school seniors would long remember:

> And I think that our philosophy in this department (at least for a
> number of us) is the big *moment*, that moment that will hang with
> them where they had to work hard and they had to be able to produce
> something of quality in front of a real audience in a real manner.

Over the following year, Jake developed curriculum that would not only prepare students for their exhibitions, but would also engage them in similar "moments" of deep engagement. I visited his classroom in 1998 on one of those days, in which his students were reenacting the debates of several key Supreme Court cases, as described in the following narrative.

A PICTURE OF PRACTICE: SUPREME COURT DEBATES

It is 8:03 a.m. on a rainy Friday in early May. Jake's twelfth-grade history students are filling a large conference room. Several of the girls are wearing jackets and skirts and a few of the boys are wearing white button-down shirts and dark pants. A table, surrounded by a number of gray chairs, has been placed in front of the blackboard at the front of the room. Students begin to sit in the chairs and pull up to the table, talking quietly. A few other students settle at the two smaller tables facing their peers.

Jake raps a judge's gavel and begins class: "Thank you for coming today," he says to his students, "I think you will enjoy hearing this case. I have talked with both sides and I am sure that they are prepared. You will need to follow the arguments in this case carefully. The Supreme Court has changed its mind several times on this issue. We will start with the State of California, who will give the facts of the case."

Jake's students are about to argue *People v. Woody*, a First Amendment case involving the free exercise of religion. Woody, a Native American, had been arrested and charged with possession of an illegal drug—peyote—the use of which, he argued, was fundamental to his religious practices. Jake and the other students at the front table will play the roles of Supreme Court justices.

Nalini, dressed smartly in a black pantsuit, walks to the podium, placing a notebook in front of her. "These are the facts of the case," she said confidently. "This drug, peyote, is illegal in the State of California. We feel that the law is the law—the law applies to everyone, no matter what." In 2–3 minutes, she gives a detailed, well-supported description of the case of the man found with peyote.

Jake raises his hand and says he has a few questions. "Were the police there? Was there any problem obtaining warrants?" A student representing Woody, Janice, replied, "Yes, the police were there and there were no problems." Robert, a student on the bench of justices, asks if the search took place on a reservation and the students respond that it did not. Jake then suggests, "Let's move on to the opening arguments. We'll start again with the State of California."

Bradley stands and walks to the podium. "Good morning. We represent the People in this case. In our society we see drug-related problems all the time. There are many reasons why drugs are illegal. . . . " He argues that other Native American tribes have seen the dangers of peyote and have criminalized its use. For instance, the Apache tribe recognized that they were often fighting under the influence of the drug. "The Apaches blamed the peyote," he explains. Bradley cites a case, *Employment Division of Oregon v. Smith,* in which a person was denied health benefits after being fired for failing a drug test, who then claimed the drugs were for religious reasons, and who lost the case. He asks rhetorically, "What's the difference between a Parkside High School student smoking pot for religious reasons and Woody smoking peyote for religious reasons?" Bradley continues with his argument for several more minutes, referring to precedent cases and posing provocative questions about the potential for anyone to claim—sincerely or insincerely—drug use for religious purposes.

The remainder of the period continues with the counsel representing the Defendants in the case at the podium. The students refer to precedent cases in which religious groups had been granted exceptions in the law, such as not requiring school attendance after 12 years of age for Amish youth, and allowing children under 18 to drink wine during Catholic communion. Students have a few minutes for clarifying questions, and then the Justices spend the remaining 15 minutes of this class period conferring with one another to decide the case while the other students write their opinions. The room is quiet. Attentively, the students lean over their notebooks.

Jake and I met after this class for a brief interview. He was thrilled with how the class went. Although he had started off the class by introducing the day and the plans, he delegated himself to the background thereafter and his students were clearly in charge that day. The students who presented were articulate, well-prepared, and had clearly done their research. He noted with pleasure that the students representing the State of California must have conducted some additional research the previous night in order to strengthen their case. He explained that they had found information about the Apache tribe that he not known himself, and buttressed their argument. He felt that each group had researched carefully, and presented their arguments cohesively and persuasively. The quiet and present engagement of the whole class as they listened to their peers suggested that all students felt a deep interest and involvement in their work and that of their classmates—just the kind of "moment" Jake envisioned.

Jake continued to explain that he felt that these moments represent the heart of teaching and the focus of his vision: "I just love that, those moments when they're not screwin' around and they're 'on,' and it matters to them. And you kind of think, 'This is what it's all about.'" He concluded, "I'll be happy all weekend because those cases were really well done." He observed that this particular day is close to the best he can accomplish, given the current conditions—and constraints—of his school context. He reflected with satisfaction, "I think this is as good as I can do. Maybe that's not great, but maybe it's something worth being proud of. . . . For me, in terms of my vision, this is pretty close to what I can do. I mean, this is *good.*"

At other times, however, his vision felt quite far away from his classroom activities. In fact, Jake described the very next class meeting of the same students—a debriefing on those supreme court debates—as "nothing special." He also identified a few things he might do differently next time.

Yet this juxtaposition of the remarkable and the ordinary does not dishearten Jake. Rather, he thinks of his teaching as including apex moments and those commonplace days:

> I would be proud . . . if anybody came in and saw [Friday]. And today [Monday] if somebody just popped in and saw it out of context, then it would be, "Okay, it's fine, there was some good stuff." . . . But it's not like you'd put that [today] out there as a model...but if you see it, I think, as a follow-up and part of the puzzle that has to be there, it's a piece that you have to deal with.

In a way, it seems as if Jake thinks of the approach to these apex moments as the ascent of a series of mountain ranges. Jake might spend days, weeks, or even months scaffolding students' understanding, sitting in committee meetings, or working with individual students. Those days are the climb toward the peak of a mountain. After a long time scaling the mountain, Jake reaches the apex of the climb in a "moment" in which everything he and the students have been working toward coalesces. As Jake explains, "It happens in certain flashes at certain moments and certain assignments, certain days, where you see things go right. This does happen." But then he descends again, and must build all over again toward another moment.

This is not to say that Jake never experiences frustration, doubts, or disappointments during those descents, or that he never lacks motivation. He cautions:

> I'm not immune to feeling really bad when those . . . moments don't go well, when you build it all up and you prepare for this and then the students aren't ready or they can't give the presentation or they don't know very much. . . .There are days when I wake up and think, "Oh, it's not going to be a very interesting lesson today."

Yet Jake observes, "having a sense of something bigger coming, or working toward something bigger gets me through those times. Because I don't really have a feeling that those days are that significant in the larger picture." Because Jake has a vision that encompasses ordinary days as well as uplifting moments, he feels he is able to "work through" the inevitable feelings of frustration and discouragement from setbacks and disappointments that accompany the daily routine.

In addition, Jake also points out that he understands that his ability to enact his vision is intimately tied to his school context. In particular, Jake observed that an unwieldy student-teacher ratio, lack of time to reflect and improve the unit, along with limited opportunities to interact and collaborate with colleagues constrained his ability to move still closer to his vision. So while he emphasized that he was quite proud of the way his students argued the Supreme Court cases, he qualified that his work (and that of his students) still only represented what was possible given his current context.

Thus it is with the knowledge of such constraints that Jake judges his work. In fact, he reflected a few months later, "I think at that particular moment, I was very happy with what had happened. [But] it's not as good as I can do if things were changed and I was working in a different situation." This image of practice and his reflection upon it reveals that Jake constantly thinks about the relationship between what is possible given his particular school context and his teaching situation and his ideals. He concluded, "In terms of vision, I see things that could be better. I'm not satisfied with saying that's the best I'm ever going to do."

Indeed, Jake felt that his understanding of what he could accomplish and the means to it was growing. "More and more I see my role within my classroom [as] kind of a microenvironment—inside my classroom as being half my job; and then the school as a whole, the macro sort of institution, as being the other half of my job." He believed that he was learning that it was very important that his vision looked "beyond the classroom" and that he could "see the bigger picture." In fact, rather than seeing his vision solely focused upon certain achievements in his particular classroom, he senses that his vision traverses the classroom and the school. He concludes, waving a hand at his written vision description: "Here's what I want to do in the *classroom*, but very much also, I'd like to be a part of this sort of *school*."

TAKING INSPIRATION FROM COLLEAGUES: YEAR TWO AT PARKSIDE

During the following year at Parkside, Jake began to feel that there was more that he could do with the kinds of "moments" he was attempting to shape for his students. He began to wonder whether there was a way to get his students out of the classroom and into the community. He began to feel that the kinds of moments toward which he was scaffolding needed to be even *more* powerful. He wanted them to be so significant that their learning would transfer to situations out of school.

Several of his own experiences helped foster this sense that he could craft his curriculum to have an even greater impact upon his students. He chose to attend some conferences on service learning and heard students reflect upon their experiences. He commented, "Hearing students who've been through those experiences talk about it has been really powerful because they could articulate *why* it was important to them long after it was over." He was also inspired by a new Parkside teacher who had obtained a grant at his previous school to study the swimming patterns of fish in a local stream, and the students were very engaged because the state would be actually using the data they gathered. The teacher had thoughtfully coordinated the project with the art teacher (who engaged the students in observational drawings of the fish, for example) and the physical education teacher (who obtained bikes for the students to ride to the local stream). Jake found the authentic aspects of the projects meaningful for students and was inspired by the close collaboration among teachers and by the purposeful integration of their curriculum. Finally, he learned about a program called Sojourn to the Past, which was a conference in Washington, D.C. that students attend. A fellow teacher in Jake's district had been taking students on the tour and had also developed a set of stops to historical civil rights sites along the way. Jake was particularly impressed by the students' responses to the experience: "Students who came back from that experience were different people after 10 days. . . .They were talking about wanting to start a student nonviolent group, working on political issues, and meeting with people. They wanted to do all this stuff ,and they had tremendous energy, and you could tell this wasn't going to go away."

Jake's brief but powerful encounters with these workshops and conferences were not simply the result of chance or luck. Jake noted that he always selected his professional development experiences in light of his vision. As he explained, "You don't have that much time. I'm really picky about what I'm doing." He commented that, for example, he was supposed to be training in technology because his school has a digital initiative, but "I've ignored that stuff . . . I can't see how that is going to change the way I teach." Jake purposely did not participate, choosing other professional development activities he feels are more fitting with his own vision. "I try to *focus*," he emphasizes.

Jake reflected that actually hearing from those teachers and their students helped expand his vision even more in terms of what he felt he could do with his own students: "Just to see that other people can do that is to know that it can be done." He explained that he appreciated the challenges and time needed to craft those kinds of experiences, but also noted that "I'm the type who thinks, *well, shoot, let's do that.*"

At the same time, he continued to express his understanding of and appreciation for the work that grounds such apex experiences. "You have to lay a lot of ground . . . a lot of the foundation is building up to the moment that they are out there. You can't do that stuff very often. It's not realistic. [But] over time, they are moments that become very important."

Jake immediately put his learning and inspiration to work. Over the summer and the following year, Jake and a fellow English teacher (with whom he had developed the Senior Exhibitions) planned and developed an integrated humanities Social Action Academy that was designed to take place over the course of 2 years—involving juniors and seniors in a sequential, 2-year curriculum. The Academy would involve students in exploring the notions of disenfranchised people and divisions in the country, as well as possibilities to bring people together and heal divisions. In the early spring Jake and his colleague would take the students on the sojourn and in the late spring would engage the students in a service learning project. Jake spoke with excitement about his plans to start off the year with a voter registration project, integrating powerful books such as *One Flew Over the Cuckoo's Nest* (to address "what one voice can do"). Jake planned to deal with economics issues through the lens of equity or inequity. He was thrilled about the possibilities and commented, "The vision . . . is definitely creeping into everything that I teach."

At the end of the first year of the Social Action Academy, Jake reflected that it had been a "really good year." Despite some "bumpy" elements, he explained that he had felt closer to his vision than ever. He noted that students themselves wrote an Academy constitution, that students had taken over many of the decisions of the course, and that there was "definitely a sense of community." He felt that the civil rights trip and the social action project had truly felt to him like the kinds of unique and lasting learning experiences his students would continue to build upon. He commented that this experience had led him to feel very positive about the possibilities for his vision to be enacted: "I am most optimistic about what could be done in a [large comprehensive] school like Parkside."

Yet Jake also felt that for him to feel even closer to his vision, the school needed to continue to grow and change. And, despite Jake's experiences of success and his sense of momentum in the classroom, he noted that as a school, Parkside was not making as many "steps forward" as he hoped. Thus, with mixed feelings of regret and care for Parkside but also tremendous excitement, he decided to leave Parkside High School at the end of his fifth year there. He felt he had found an opportunity to work in just the sort of school that might enable him to get even closer to that vision.

OPPORTUNITIES TO STRETCH VISION: THE MOVE TO CENTRAL CITY

Jake had learned about a small alternative school that was in development and would be opening its doors in the fall in a low-income community not far from Parkside. The school would be designed to serve the children in that community, a primarily Latino and African American population. The plan was to offer small class sizes (no more than 20 students per class), advisory groups of 15 with the same faculty member over 4 years, a strong emphasis upon parent and community connections and communication, research-based curriculum that focused upon both basic skills and higher order critical thinking, and an emphasis upon reform-based practices.

Believing that this might be a context in which he could achieve some of the schoolwide elements of his vision, Jake applied for a job and was offered a position. He accepted with mixed feelings. Noting what a "difficult" decision it was, he explained that his "heart lay with the comprehensive high school" and that he felt that he really needed to do all he could to make large public high schools better. Yet he was also immensely excited about what he viewed as the ample possibilities at Central City. He explained that what drew him most powerfully to this school was the "opportunity to enrich my vision."

Jake emphasized that his vision played a "huge part" in his decision. He explained that he viewed being on the ground floor in helping to plan and develop this school as an incredible opportunity to be a part of helping a school "do what I think schools can do." Jake was to be coteaching the ninth-grade humanities courses with another teacher who specialized in English. He would have advisory groups of students with whom he would work closely. Jake was extremely excited about the potential to develop curriculum that would draw upon local community issues and would hence become a more "authentic" and real-world course of study for the students.

In particular, he felt he could put to work (with even more freedom) his growing imaginings of a curriculum organized around projects that were deeply connected to the needs and issues at play in the local community. He and his colleagues were envisioning a progression of projects that would move from "self to group to community." So, for example, the students would start with developing their autobiographies, then move to a group study that would be informed by psychology and history, and then to a community project that would be informed by sociology, history, and ethics. Jake was driven particularly by the idea of students' work being authentic and important to others in their local area—that the students would be able to make a contribution to their own community and it would be understood, appreciated, and valued. He said with anticipation: "Students going out and doing things that are important—as I hope that happens—it's part of my vision." Furthermore, he was also eager to encounter ideas and possibilities he had not yet been able to imagine and felt that the school had that potential to help him develop and expand his vision: "It's definitely going to stretch the way I think about what's possible."

Jake commented that he welcomed the opportunities to refine and revise his vision: "I not only have to sharpen the *focus* of what I want to do, but I am also really open to fine-tuning and revising my vision." Jake also felt thrilled to be a part of this reforming school and felt that the context within which he could try to attain his own goals was really ideal. He reflected, "I can't imagine a better opportunity to achieve [my vision]," concluding that "this is my dream job."

NEW CHALLENGES: BALANCING A FOCUS
ON STUDENTS AND SUBJECT

Yet even though it was Jake's "dream job," now it seemed that the "moments" that had previously sustained him were not enough. Reflecting on his first year at Central City the following summer, Jake explained that it was a very challenging year. Despite the ideal circumstances in which he was teaching, he reflected that he "felt very far" from his vision. "There were times in my classroom when it didn't look right at all."

In particular, helping his students achieve well in his classroom was "much more difficult than I thought it would be. The process of getting them to be prepared was so much harder and required so much more energy than what I had to worry about before." He had focused on "moments" by engaging students in written projects like the autobiographies he had planned (which they presented to public judges), in a group project designing a video that documented an issue in the community, and in a public debate. "We planned the curriculum toward working students toward these peak moments. . . . Pushing students to higher levels and written work, and projects, and the next time they feel like they can do that and you can set the bar higher." While he felt that the kids ultimately did "wonderful work," he also felt that "getting there was so hard that we wouldn't have done it again that way."

Jake noted that he had felt that his vision "would be successful with any group of students," yet he found that his instruction was not working well for this group. "They didn't know what to do with the unstructured time, so it was a lot of chasing them down and getting them to do things." At times, he began to worry that his vision was not working for his students: "It's possible that it's not worth it if the 'getting there' is so difficult. I was torn. Because still you want to throw them into this engaging curriculum and have them create things and do things, and that will get them to behave the way you want them to, as opposed to training them to behave correctly before you get them into the project." Jake resolved that he had to adapt his curriculum to provide even more structure and support for this set of students to achieve well: "We had to structure the process of getting to the project better."

Jake emphasized that ultimately his vision did not change, but he did come to understand that the means to attain it—for this new group of students—needed to be even more clearly delineated:

The big vision . . . has stayed the same for what I want the kids to do and the kind of experiences I wanted them to have in class. But I really had to rethink how you prepared kids for those kinds of things, and how you structured them. I knew that. But I didn't *really* know how much different it would be, and how challenging it would be to get them to become students.

Jake's experiences echo those of Andrea and Kelly (see Chapters 2 and 3)—moving to a new school, having to learn about a new set of students (particularly those with less strong educational backgrounds)—and led him to similar questions about the appropriateness of vision and how best to continue to maintain his high standards and his commitment to his ideals. And it led him to seek ways to meet his vision through learning more about his students and restructuring the process by which he attained his vision.

Like Kelly and Andrea, Jake also reflected that being so far from his vision sometimes made him question his ability as a teacher: "It makes you rethink how good you are, and whether you're a good teacher." Yet he noted that having had experiences of success with students in the past helped reassure him: "I'm very glad I went into it with 11 years of teaching under my belt."

While before it was the "moments" that sustained him, at this point in his career, outsiders helped keep him afloat and convince him that his ideals were possible. Jake felt that having fellow educators and colleagues who periodically visited helped provide some confirmation that they were making progress. He ultimately was able to hold on to what he imagined:

We had people come in every few months who said that the kids were so much better, and I didn't see that. But I had enough sense to think that those people were right, and we must be improving. So I didn't jettison all the things I believed in, but I had to rethink how I got those things that happened.

The following year, Jake and his colleagues refined and reshaped the curriculum. Jake continued to press ahead, spurred both by his history of accomplishment as well as the understanding that there is still much to be attained. He acknowledged that "there's that part of you that wants to rush, [a feeling of] 'let's get this going' . . . 'cause I want to see it happen. . . . And so I don't want to lag. I want to keep pushing us."

THE ROLE OF CREATIVE TENSION

Jake's vision serves as a source of deep motivation and commitment. His sense of how far he has to go when he compares his vision to his daily practice propels him to tinker constantly with his practice, to seek new experiences that might enable him to make progress toward his vision, and even to switch schools so that he has further opportunities to learn in order to better enact his vision. Senge (1990) has explained that the juxtaposition of vision and current reality can generate a powerful drive to learn in order to bridge the gap between vision and reality—which Senge captures in the term *creative tension*. Jake's language reflects this sense of creative tension over and over: as he talks about that "part of you that wants to rush, that 'let's get this going' . . .'cause I want to see it happen" or when he emphasizes that "I don't want to lag; I want to keep pushing us." Jake also reveals the effects of creative tension when he talks about how "energizing" it is to move to a place where he feels closer to his vision and how "exciting" it is to be able to meet with his colleagues and plan new curriculum.

Consistently comparing vision to practice might be discouraging and disheartening for some teachers. Yet Jake, at least most of the time, enjoys satisfaction with his work and fulfillment as a teacher. Indeed, he commented at one point, "Not matching up to a vision is better than not having a vision." Jake was able to maintain his commitment to teaching and find satisfaction in his work, even when he is not "matching up" to his vision at all times, because he considers the movement toward his vision to be an "ongoing process." The ordinary days are not seen as a disappointment, but as a necessary part of the journey.

Jake seems to carry his appreciation for the episodic nature of vision over to the crafting of his career. Just as one can see him thoroughly and carefully designing his curriculum to support and move toward those "moments" of deep student engagement, one can recognize a parallel in his approach to his own career. Jake's career choices have been extremely purposeful and deliberate. He has a clear vision of what he wants to accomplish, and he has used his vision thoughtfully and intentionally to select a path of opportunities—from selecting schools, as Andrea and Kelly did, to choosing professional development—that will enable him to get closer to what he thinks he can do with his teaching and for his students. Each time, he has sought out and developed a position that would help him grow professionally, stretch his potential, and push him farther along toward his own sense of the "possible." At the same time, he constantly reminds himself of the nature of the journey—that it takes time, that it may have setbacks, and that his work is not always ideal—although there may be those *moments*.

CHAPTER 5

Teaching with a Social Purpose

When I first met Carlos, he was a student teacher, teaching history at Sandhill High School, a large high school in northern California's Bay Area. Carlos explained that he had past experience at Sandhill that provided a critical means of understanding his vision and his teaching:

> I'll have to start from the past in order to explain my vision. The school that I'm student teaching in now is actually the school that I went to, and it's the community that I grew up in. I grew up in the same community where a lot of my students are now.

Carlos described himself as "always" thinking about his community, adding that "my whole purpose of even becoming a teacher . . . my bigger goal . . . was to help the community." Teaching in a community like Sandhill had long been a professional and personal goal for him. Carlos believed that such a setting was essential for him in order to make progress toward his vision. He had pushed hard to be placed at Sandhill High School during his student teaching semester, despite the objections of the faculty at his teacher education program who worried about his ability to change roles from student to teacher. He was planning to continue to teach at Sandhill as a full-time teacher of history once he graduated from his teacher preparation program.[1]

Carlos explained that his vision centered upon helping the Latino students in his classroom (and school) raise their expectations about themselves and their work, care deeply about their schooling, and ultimately go on to higher education. The current poor performance of Latino students at Sandhill deeply concerned Carlos, and he reflected that "my vision is to change that: to get the students at Sandhill High School to change their vision about what they want." He explained that he wanted to "motivate the students to care about their schooling."

More broadly, he believed that helping more Latino students attend college will ultimately improve the entire community. Carlos felt strongly that education is the most important avenue toward new opportunities and possibilities for the Latino community. He observed, "I've seen that education is the way that any community has improved in this country. Rarely anything else gets a whole community out of poverty, out of the worst paying jobs. So . . . to come up economically you have to come up in education and politically as well." While Carlos was very optimistic about the outcomes of his hopes and dreams, he acknowledged that it could take years—even decades—for his vision of Latino youth becoming academically successful as a community to come to pass. He commented, "Maybe later on when they have kids they'll understand those issues, and maybe they'll be better at helping their students do better . . . I think maybe it will take a couple of generations to happen."

Carlos explained that he often discusses this vision of community improvement through education with his own students. He felt that it was critical that they understood what his ultimate goals were in teaching for himself and for them. As he explained, "That's explicit to my students. They know my purpose of coming back and teaching is because I want to help my community. They all know this. It's one of the first things I tell them."

Carlos reflected that the opportunity to teach at Sandhill had enabled him to come "full circle" after graduating from an elite university:

> So I guess I'm coming full circle now and I like that. I guess the . . . whole notion of time being more circular in the Latino community than linear [attracts] me. It's not one thing and then the other, and then you forget about the past. You are always thinking about the past and you are trying to hope for the future.

Carlos's vision stands out as a social vision: It is a vision of the development of an entire community. While he has a strong sense of how his classroom and his teaching fit into this broader vision, his vision extends far beyond one class or even one school. Carlos's vision is also indisputably a very distant one. It involves a particular population gaining more economic, political, and educational access. It is a dream that he acknowledges may take decades or even generations. How does Carlos make progress toward a vision when attainment of it is so far away, and continue to press on?

In contrast to Jake, Kelly, and Andrea (see Chapters 2, 3, and 4), the context that helps sustain Carlos is not a classroom or a school. Rather, it is the larger community of which he is a part. Recent research has helped demonstrate the essential ways in which context shapes teachers' work—influencing the way that teachers feel about their students, their practice, their school, and even their profession. For instance, McLaughlin and Talbert (1993) found that even within districts, some school contexts can support teachers in their efforts to learn new practices that engage students in challenging learning experiences, while other school contexts foster discouragement and cynicism among teachers and students, leading to student failure.

However, how supportive or unsupportive a school is, is a matter of perception. What an outsider might view as a particularly difficult or impoverished teaching context may be quite different from a teacher's point of view. In Carlos's case, his school was large, the dropout rate was high, and particularly relevant to Carlos's concerns, Latino students were not particularly well supported. Regular articles in the education section of the local paper often criticized Sandhill's inability to prepare students well. Frequent turnover plagued the faculty and administration, and the principalship turned over several times while Carlos was teaching there. Many teachers might not persevere in a school like this.

Yet despite these problems Carlos actually viewed this school as a necessary—and in many ways ideal—setting in which to work toward his vision. In order to enact his vision, he needed to work with students like himself and give them the benefit of his own experiences. He chose Sandhill High School because of the high population of Latino students—that was where the children were. Indeed, the context that really mattered to Carlos was not really Sandhill High School itself, but the students who were members of his larger cultural community.

Finally, the source of Carlos's vision shapes the relationship between subject and students—and the ways in which he focuses more upon students than subject. Carlos based his vision upon his unwavering belief that education can help people like himself. He commented, "What drives me is just wanting to see other people enjoy the benefits that I have enjoyed. I enjoy how knowledge has changed me . . . and I want that for other people."

Carlos felt that Latino students could and should become "insiders" in the educational community. Yet in many ways he felt like an outsider during his high school educational career. Up until Carlos was in tenth grade, he was in this country illegally. Many of his teachers, however, assumed he was a citizen. Some of them, without knowing about his situation, expressed beliefs that illegal immigrants were not welcome at the school. Carlos recalled that gradually he began to agree, and he began to wish he were not Latino and "more White."

Furthermore, he felt he was learning a Eurocentric view of history which he felt had made him question the strength, power, and ability of people like himself. He was frequently the only Latino student in his AP courses. He recalled, "I felt horrible . . . about my own ethnicity." Now he feels strongly that "I never want any student to feel that their race, culture, and experiences are not valuable: I want my students to realize that they have a great heritage, just like the European heritage is great. And we have the genes to do great things in our lives, too."

CARLOS'S VISION

In the description of his vision that Carlos wrote while a student teacher, the central image is that of Latino students posting just as many letters of college acceptance on the wall of the school as the White students do. Underlying this image is his focus upon making sure that an equal number of Latino students and White students enjoy academic success. He observes,

> If you look at proportions, if everything would be right, it would be fifty-fifty . . . fifty percent of the White students would be up there and fifty percent of the Latino students would be up there and then that would be fine. But I don't see fifty-fifty.

While Carlos emphasizes that his focus is upon the academic success of his Latino students, he notes that his vision encompasses all students and that he imagines this kind of success for all his students: "I know that I always focus a lot on the Latinos, but whenever there's a student in my classroom I'll work my hardest to help them achieve, no matter what."

Carlos describes his role as a teacher in his ideal classroom as both facilitator and motivator. On the one hand, he envisioned himself tapping into students' innate curiosities and interests, helping them think about things they had not thought about before, and facilitating their learning. On the other hand, he imagined his role as fostering students' interest in continued learning. Carlos hoped he could help students develop initiative regarding their own education, in which they "come to a point where they're going to become active in the school and ask what classes they're taking and if those classes are going to get them to college."

Carlos envisions his students graduating high school with a record of success, obtaining higher education, and then "becoming something important." In fact, Carlos imagines many of his students becoming teachers themselves. He asserts, "I definitely, definitely see a lot of my students going on to college and becoming something . . . important. And even some of them [becoming] teachers." Furthermore, Carlos hopes to see his students returning to his neighborhood, educated and highly motivated, increasing the ranks of those committed to community improvement and, in turn, further fueling development. He sees them becoming "people who care about that community and . . . want to see it improve."

Therefore, in his ideal classroom students are part of a strong community in which they are "learning to help others" as well as their own families:

> In my ideal classroom . . . my students care about doing well because they have a higher purpose. They are no longer concerned about trivial

things . . . but understand that they need to learn as much as they can because they are an important link in their family's chain.

Carlos describes the source of his vision as his own personal experiences and beliefs, explaining that it has evolved over time "from seeing how my people have been working in what you would call the worst jobs there are in the United States. A lot of my people are not educated, so there's [few] options for them to do another job." He began to imagine how his community could improve, and felt that education was the most powerful force he could envision.

Carlos finds support knowing that his vision is not only about community, but it is also shared by a broader community of his peers. He explained that while he was at his university, he found other Latino students who voiced the same vision:

Just being an undergraduate here, just a lot of discussions I had with other friends . . . you really get a sense of where the needs are and what you really need to do. And a lot of my friends who I would say share a similar vision [are] in different fields. [Even] the friends of mine who are in engineering have similar visions.

ELABORATING A COMMUNITY VISION: FIRST YEARS AT SANDHILL

The Right Context

One of the first steps Carlos took in order to work toward his vision was to select a setting in which he believed that he could begin to attain it. Even as a student teacher, he had been strategic about how to get closer to his vision and had insisted upon being placed at Sandhill for his student teaching semester in spite of the objections of his teacher education faculty. Then he sought and was offered a full-time position teaching history for the following year, which was just what he had hoped for. As he explained, "My vision is to go back to Sandhill, and I want to have an impact at the school. I want to raise the standards at the school. I want to motivate the students to care about their schooling."

Carlos felt that the context of Sandhill High School was in many ways a perfect setting for him to make progress toward his vision in his first years of teaching. It offered the opportunity to work directly in the community in which he had grown up, and enabled him to begin making a contribution to that community. Furthermore, having grown up in the same community as his students, even attending Sandhill himself as a student, enabled him to make powerful connections to his students' lives and experiences.

Carlos immediately leveraged those similarities with his students as a means to make connections to them. For example, during the first few months of his first year teaching there, he brought in a picture of his younger brother photographed with a friend to share with the students to help them get to know him. One of his students remarked with surprise that the friend with Carlos's younger brother in the picture was *his* own brother. Carlos felt that incident represented an important illustration of the kind of connection the students could make with him. That photograph helped them see that he was a part of their community. Through recognizing such similarities, perhaps his students could better listen to his experiences and learn from him.

In addition, he could occasionally see his students informally outside of class. During his first few years at Sandhill, he sometimes played pickup basketball with several students who lived nearby. He considered those moments to be opportunities to respond to students' concerns from class, to motivate them, to answer questions, and to encourage them in their academic pursuits.

Identifying Constraints on His Students

Even in his first year of teaching, Carlos had already begun to explore what was constraining his Latino students' academic success. He noted that all his students were extremely bright and able. Yet most of them appeared to lack the confidence to "go on." He felt that "no matter how much I say that they can do it," many would not be able to make the sustained, serious effort necessary for them to pursue higher education. Finally, he observed that few students were imagining themselves attending college: "A lot of these students are just looking forward to working right after high school . . . my students just don't *see* themselves going to college right after high school." Clearly, they did not yet have the vision of academic success he dreamed for them.

During my first visit to his classroom, Carlos pointed out Roberto, a ninth grader in his class who he felt was quite bright but did not muster enough hard work to maintain good grades. Carlos surmised that the reason for Roberto's lackluster effort was that Roberto did not make the connection between his effort in school and the kinds of coursework and grades one has to have to get to college. Carlos commented, "There are a lot of students like that, there's a lot of Latinos like that [who are not making the efforts they need to] because they don't see the steps that are required to get to college."

Carlos was beginning to feel that he needed to do more than just motivate and cajole his students into extending more effort into their schoolwork. He believed that part of the reason for his Latino students' lack of effort was that they didn't have the practical knowledge they needed in order to prepare for college. He decided that he needed to teach his students that information directly and provide them the planning skills they needed.

Carlos immediately set to work on this problem. He developed a curriculum that he called the College Preparation Unit to teach in the late spring in all of his social studies classes. The curriculum was designed to enable his students to learn and understand the choices and effort they would need to pursue in order to attain higher education. The unit involved students in taking personality and job interest tests, reading about and identifying jobs that were of interest to them, discussing college requirements, looking at high school courses and how they would (or would not) fulfill various college requirements (down to the specifics of what was required for a community college, 4-year college, public university, and private university), reviewing transcripts, learning how to calculate a GPA, and developing their own high school course schedule for 4 years. Carlos also arranged for guest speakers, such as the high school guidance counselor, to talk to his students about the college application process.

Carlos noted that with a unit like this he hoped to help his students begin to develop some vision of their own future. He says that often his students want to help their own families but they choose short-term solutions like long hours at jobs that make some money but also take away from their ability to do well in school. He worries that "they're not thinking that maybe they could help *more* if they did really well in school."

In the spring of Carlos's first year as a full-time teacher, I visited his classroom to observe 2 days of his teaching during the College Preparation Unit. A narrative based on my observation follows.

A Picture of Practice: The College Preparation Unit

Carlos watches the students file in and tells them that he is waiting for them to settle down. "Uno, dos . . ." he counts, while waiting. Then he jokes, "Oh no, I can't speak Spanish."[2] He starts to count, this time in English, "One, two, three four five . . . " He then says, "I want to remind you guys, a lot of you . . . your averages have gone up a great deal. The average in this class has now gone up . . . a lot of you have turned in work that you owed." Carlos also reminds them that they have a project due on Friday that they must turn in then if they want extra credit. He reviews aloud the criteria he has developed for a good project. Otavio, often talkative in class, complains jokingly that Carlos is too inexperienced to know what he wants for their work: "You rookie!" he exclaims. Carlos responds, "Yeah, but I'm a rookie from *Stanford*."

The bell rings, and Carlos asks one of his students, Lily, to pass out a photocopied newspaper article entitled, "Today's Diplomas Don't Mean Much to Employers." Carlos begins with the question about what the article's title means. "Why is this? Everybody tells you that diplomas do mean a lot, but this article says they don't. What does the author mean?" Ottie says that he thinks that the author means that people get away with doing poor work in school, adding that, "You need training, knowledge to know what you're going to do." Carlos nods and elaborates, "You're saying that if a student is just getting a D, they are not really learning the basics." Ottie then says, "This author says we are the only place where we give a diploma for sitting in a chair. I think that's true." Carlos looks at all the students and asks, "What do you all think about that?" Some students nod their heads in assent.

He then asks, "So do you guys know what you need to do to graduate? Let's review what you need to know . . . " He lists the years of high school at the top of a graph, and the subject areas down the side. For each year, he asks students what they think they need to take in each area. "How many years of English do you need?" he asks. He goes over the requirements for every year of high school in order to graduate.

Carlos then says, "OK, now . . . if you want to go to *college*, you need 3 to 4 years of science instead of 2." He adds, "And to go to a UC, you need to take precalculus." He reminds them, "It is possible to catch up, if you use your summers wisely." He urges, "So you understand how important it is to pass all your courses or to make up classes if you need to make them up—so you can go to the college you want to or the university you want."

Carlos then says he wants to share something with them. Freshman year he took "Algebra .5," did really well in the class and the teacher urged him to go to Algebra II. "What did I do?" He explains, "I did this." He turns around and looks back over his shoulder: "I turned around and I saw all my friends and I didn't want to leave them. So I said, 'No, that's OK.'" Instead, he told them, he went into Algebra I the next year and the teacher told him immediately that he should not be in the class, but he now had to take it anyway. It was an easy A, but he knew he should have taken it the year before. He then realized he needed to take more classes in order to go to college, and he ended up having to take two classes of math his junior year. He reflects, "Because I was wanting to be with my friends, I had to take doubled-up classes."

The students ask what his friends are doing now. He says that some of them don't have jobs. Carlos moves back to the issue at hand about colleges, "So, I want you to understand what you need to graduate and what you need to get into college. Do you understand that?" The students chorus that they do. Carlos asks if anyone can name some of the branches of the University of California. No one responds, so he says, "UC Davis, UCLA, UCSB, UC Irvine." He says that they are harder to get into than the others. He adds that there are also private universities, which have the most competitive admissions policies.

A student comments, "Yeah, you need to be smart to get into them!" Carlos responds, "I didn't say *anything* about being smart." He tells the class that often he hears students saying that someone who got an A is "smarter" than the person who got a B. But that kind of comment is a "cop-out." The person is not getting As "because she is smart, it's because she is *doing her work.*"

For Carlos, all the decisions about what to do in his classroom and his curriculum have less to do with how he envisions his subject matter than with how he envisions his students—what he thinks they need, what he has learned about them, and what he dreams for their future. He explained, "I want that college experience for every one of them. And if I'm not helping them get there, then how could I say that I'm doing the right thing?" To that end, Carlos's teaching focused upon helping his students get a "better sense of the path of how it is that they get to graduate from high school, and get into college." He recalled that as a student himself, "I knew that there was high school and there was college, but I didn't see the path that I needed to take." He explained, "By the end of this unit, I want them to be able to look back at their grades and say, 'Whoa . . . I've got a 2.0 and according to all of this I need to get at least a 3.0' . . . they can tell themselves, 'Well, I have to really kick it into gear next year and the following year.'"

The other striking element of Carlos's practice is his emphasis upon effort and drive. He wants his students to understand that being successful has less to do with innate "smarts" and much more to do with the amount of effort one can muster. He emphasizes careful planning, informed decision making, and a view of the future that might mean ignoring peer pressure and choosing more difficult options.

Finally, Carlos's continued use of connections to his students to help them learn is evident in his practice. He tells them a story about his own high school experiences, designed to help them see how a poor decision on his part came to haunt him later in his high school career. He hopes that these kinds of resonating stories will make sense to them and will enable them not only to see themselves in the stories but also to learn from them.

Developing Additional Curriculum to Fit with Vision

In addition to developing the College Preparation Unit, Carlos was also imagining what he could do over the next few years to get closer to his vision.

He felt that he needed to develop courses that would help his Latino students understand and appreciate their own cultural and historical background. He commented that he could clearly envision himself teaching those topics: "I see myself teaching a course in Chicano studies or Latino studies . . . .I see myself leading this thing and I see students coming and talking to me." Again, Carlos was making choices based not upon any particular commitment to key ideas in the subject of history, but much more upon what his students needed to learn in order to develop personally.

In fact, the following year, he created a Latin American studies course and taught it for the first time. He explained that, as he had designed it, the first part of the course focused upon learning about Latin American history in some depth; and then the second focused upon evaluating United States history from a Latino perspective. As he explained, "I think these students need to understand where Latin America lies in relation to the rest of the world, and how Latino Americans have helped shape U.S. history. I feel that Latino students are not served [without such an experience] and need to learn to value and respect their own culture." Carlos described teaching courses like this as a key part of his vision:

> [In some ways, it's] the most important part of my vision. Social studies teaches toward the soul . . . it teaches where you came from. A lot of Latino students don't know where they come from. The curriculum that they've been taught focuses upon European accomplishments. I love European history and think that's important, but we still need to focus upon the other part of our heritage—the indigenous side. I tell students that we need to know about Mayan mythology as well as Greek mythology.

In light of his own experiences with history as a high school student, Carlos had come to believe that part of his role was to teach his students to take a more critical stance toward history. This meant that they needed to learn to "always question things and not always just accept them as truth, as fact." Furthermore, Carlos said that part of his emphasis on learning Latin American history had to do with helping his students see the power and possibility of people who shared their cultural heritage. An appreciation of such historical background could in turn contribute to the necessary sense of efficacy and confidence for productive lives.

At this point in his career, Carlos felt very confident that he would be able to enact at least some of his vision. In fact, when asked how he might feel if he were unable to accomplish it, he responded, "I really don't see that happening." While Carlos acknowledged the challenges of attaining his vision, in his first years he was unflinchingly positive about his ability to bridge the gap between vision and practice.

NOT JUST A VISION OF ONE CLASSROOM:
THIRD AND FOURTH YEARS AT SANDHILL

By his third year at Sandhill, Carlos had begun to think about how to extend his vision beyond his own classroom to the whole school community. He was making connections to other teachers who seemed to share his goals and dreams. He was hoping to find ways to broaden the impact of his vision at the school.

While Carlos had a vision with a very broad range encompassing his classroom, school, and community, he had not fully fleshed out what his vision might look like at the school level beyond his own classroom. But by his third year Carlos had come to an understanding quite similar to what Kelly had voiced: If the vision is not expressed in the other classrooms students encounter, students may get contradictory messages that can undermine one's goals for them. "I've realized that even though I've created this sort of atmosphere in my classroom and raised their expectations, once the kids leave my classroom they go into another classroom that has a totally different tone. That destroys what I've accomplished." One can have a greater impact upon students if the vision is consistent across classrooms: "I think there needs to be a way that it's a whole school system, and not just a 'one-classroom' experience." Carlos's insights echo those expressed by Kelly, who also had come to an understanding that one's vision may best be achieved when shared by others at a school.

To that end, Carlos started taking on leadership roles in his school. Toward the end of his second year, Carlos was invited by his principal to help develop and direct the AVID program at his school for the following year.[3] Carlos was intrigued by the possibility that he could put his vision to work with more students in more classes and in other contexts. He was excited by the program's focus upon "academically average" students, and minority and low-income students. As Carlos saw it, this was exactly the kind of population he envisioned helping.

He committed himself to making the AVID program successful. In light of his growing belief that students needed to hear similar messages across classes as well as from each other, he organized the program so that the students would all take classes together.

In his third and fourth years at Sandhill, Carlos was also learning about how to organize evidence that would support his vision. He began gathering data in his classroom that could help demonstrate how well students can do if their teachers raise expectations for them. Over those 2 years, he and his colleagues demonstrated that the students in the AVID program (who, he pointed out, were by no means the "best students" but were drawn from the "same" population as other average students in the school) gained more class credits and obtained an average GPA of 2.8 as opposed to 2.0 for mainstream freshman. Their data also showed that 90% of the students had taken Algebra I as freshman, as opposed to the standard 20% of the mainstreamed students who made that choice. Carlos explained, "The data . . . show that you can take similar kids but you create a different atmosphere for them, and they rise to those expectations."

At the end of his fourth year, Carlos remained optimistic about the possibility of attaining his vision. He was encouraged that he seemed to be making a difference beyond his own classroom. He joined forces with a group of teachers who were beginning to work on restructuring the school into smaller "academies," making him feel even more strongly that he might be able to make progress toward his vision. He envisioned having the same teachers teach the same students "so that they have common ground when they talk about students." As he saw it, "it is all to help the students and keep them from falling through the cracks."

These efforts bolstered his optimism even more. "I feel a lot better about my teaching and about the future. If I was just a classroom teacher who gets involved in one committee, I would not feel as if I have grown as much as I have. I would feel frustrated at not creating schoolwide change."

The constant interplay between his vision and his efforts to develop daily steps toward it played a central role in his sense of motivation and fulfillment. Indeed, Carlos was very positive about his ability to achieve his vision: "If things go well, I'm 2 to 3 years away from my vision. In terms of my classroom, I know what I'm doing now."

At this time, Carlos was offered a position at a nearby charter school that was designed to serve underperforming Latino students. He considered their offer carefully as he felt their school was very much "aligned with my vision" and he "would have added a lot to the staff there." Despite the fact that the school's population was primarily Latino, they were "lacking an emphasis in Latino culture," which he knew he could provide. But he ultimately turned them down, feeling as if he had many opportunities to make some progress toward his vision through his work at Sandhill High School. Even though one might think that a school that was specifically focused upon Latino students would be an even more ideal fit for Carlos and his vision, he continued to conceive of Sandhill as the right setting for him to make progress toward his vision.

A Turning Point: "My Vision Was Lost"

However, the following year represented a turning point for Carlos. Although Carlos continued to experience some success and make progress with some students, his sense of accomplishment and momentum began to dwindle. Carlos felt that he did everything he could to help his students— beyond his regular curriculum he also made extra efforts like following up on particular students' schedules to be sure they were taking the correct classes for college admittance. While there were some complaints from other teachers who felt Carlos was getting whatever he wanted for his students, he explained that "the friction didn't matter to me, because my kids were in the right classes."

Yet for the first time Carlos began to feel more concerned that the Sandhill faculty and the administration were not making a pointed enough effort to raise standards for students. Even though the AVID program was making real progress, the students' reading levels were not as high as he felt they should be. He felt as if 2 years ago they had started the discussion about low reading levels "and 2 years into the program we were still talking about it." He felt that the progress he had enjoyed in previous years was faltering: "Nothing was taking shape. Change was so slow, I felt disheartened." He began to be concerned that "it was all talk by the teachers. As soon as the talks were over, there was no implementation."

Carlos also noticed that some of the "good kids" were dropping out of AVID. In his first few years he had recognized Sandhill's lack of emphasis on high achievement as a problem but felt he could work within the culture. But he now had growing concerns that the culture of the school reinforced students' lack of achievement rather than countering it. Carlos believed that his students recognized that the school's regular curriculum was easier than that required by AVID, and the students were not in a larger environment that was conducive to such hard work and academic effort: "If the school is a ship, AVID [is designed to be like a boat] to give students a little boost so that students can make it to the destination. But I felt we were on a speedboat that was going much faster than the ship, and my students wanted to be on the cruise ship that was more fun, that was going slower."

Carlos's concerns echo those shared by Kelly when at Blackwell High School. Both Carlos and Kelly came to believe that it was very difficult to help students have alternative school experiences that were more consistent with their visions. In essence, both Carlos and Kelly were learning that it was extremely difficult to maintain their own high standards for children, as rooted in their visions, in their particular public school contexts.

For Carlos, the process of moving toward official AVID status was not only equally disheartening, but ended up dealing the final blow to his hopes and efforts. The previous year, he and his colleagues had presented to AVID officials what they felt was an accurate view of their program. They shared not only the goals they had achieved, but also highlighted some of the areas where they felt they still needed to improve. After that presentation, he and his colleagues had been granted affiliate status, which was a kind of provisional membership within the AVID organization.

The following year, he and his colleagues decided to present the successes and not to focus upon the challenges and problems. "We showed them our good things: We only had one or two kids failing all of their classes of the schools 200 students who were doing so; our kids had higher grades than the average Sandhill student; the reading level was going up faster—we had data to back these things up. And when we had the meeting with the AVID coordinator, I thought she would just give us affiliate status and [tell us to] try again next year. But she gave us official AVID status."

Surprisingly, Carlos was shocked and dismayed by this turn of events. As he put it, "Instead of making me happy, that made me angry." While official status was clearly something that would be good for the school and the program, he was extremely frustrated that the program went by what it seemed to want to hear. He felt it was hypocritical. That same night "[when] we should have been celebrating," he sent an email to the principal of the charter school who had approached him 3 years earlier. He said he would like to come and visit the school. As he explained, "I don't want to be part of something I have to cover up [and] sugar coat . . . I'd rather be straightforward and address problems."

Most of all, he felt that it was clear he was no longer able to work toward his vision. As he explained, "My vision was [becoming] lost that year. I felt I had to start all over again. If I'm going to dedicate another 5 years to something, it's too tiring to go against the grain."

Carlos's experience, like that of Kelly, Andrea, and Jake, demonstrates the profound difficulties for a teacher with high standards struggling to enact a powerful vision in a public school context. Ultimately, like his other colleagues with strong visions, Carlos chose to leave the public school. His choice had an even more complex layer of regret and disappointment, given his deep personal history at the school and the depth of his commitment to the community it served. Yet at the same time, because Carlos's vision stretched beyond the school (and he could serve his community and find students like himself elsewhere), he was able to continue to pursue it by simply moving to a new and more appropriate setting.

A BETTER SETTING FOR VISION: THE MOVE TO LINCOLN COLLEGE PREPARATORY

The principal of the new school "emailed right back" and invited Carlos to visit. Carlos toured the school and was very impressed by their commitment to college education for their primarily Latino students, and for their focus upon students who are typically unsuccessful in ordinary high school settings. He felt that with Lincoln's mission so obviously close to his vision, it seemed like an ideal fit.[4] In addition, Lincoln College Preparatory was personally "welcoming," and he sensed that they were genuinely deeply interested in him. This appealed to his own beliefs about the importance of relationships in school community—also a key element in his vision. Thus, while he was still feeling committed to Sandhill at the time, he decided to go through the interview process. He was invited to conduct a sample class for an audience of parents, students, and teachers, and recalled, "I started to want to come here so badly that I was nervous."

Soon after interviewing, Carlos was offered a position as a College Readiness teacher—just what he had been doing as part of his social studies courses at Sandhill and about as close to what he had envisioned as possible. This position involved a more challenging and heavy teaching load. At Sandhill, Carlos was responsible for teaching only two classes a day in addition to the AVID class he taught, and he had been given two preparatory periods, one for his Social Studies classes and another for AVID: "I had a ton of time." Yet at Lincoln he was going to be teaching five courses a day, as well as a tutorial class for students in need of special help. He was also not going to be working with an easier population of students. As at Sandhill, he would be teaching students unaccustomed to academic success. On top of all that, Carlos would be leaving a tenured teaching position at Sandhill and taking a thousand-dollar pay cut. Yet he was willing to make these sacrifices. These issues of salary, tenure, and course load were "not deciding factors at all." Rather, whether he could make progress toward the kinds of teaching he wanted to do was the key factor in his decision.

One year into his teaching career at Lincoln, Carlos remained impressed by a number of aspects of the school that he felt were consistent with his own vision. The principal shakes the hand of every child in the morning. The principal and the vice principal both talk about the school as something that belongs to the community. And finally, "*Everyone* talks about college."

Carlos felt that being at Lincoln was enabling him to stretch and develop his own vision. He felt recharged. As he reflected, the fit between his goals and the school's mission was wonderfully compatible. "I feel more a part of this school than I did in 4 years . . . as a high school student at Sandhill and 5 years as a teacher. In one year, I feel more a part of the community at Lincoln than I did in my entire student career and teaching career. And so now I talk about 'we we we' at Lincoln."

Indeed, he said he now felt that his vision was much closer than it had been at Sandhill. He felt that he was learning that aspects of his vision that he "knew in his heart" would work, *did* work. Elements like creating a strong community in the school and classroom, creating a sense of family in the classroom, involving parents, empowering parents—he was now seeing that "it can be done."

At the same time, Carlos recognizes that there is still tremendous work to be done to make progress toward his vision—and that of the school's. But at Lincoln, he feels intimately and deeply involved in the work: "I am a part of the groundwork, creating a curriculum for the College Readiness class."

Carlos recognizes that having a vision does not necessarily mean "getting there" immediately—or perhaps even ever arriving. It's rather constantly a destination and a reach for something challenging a bit beyond one's grasp. As he explains, "Having that vision is not like—it's not like arriving there. It's always looking ahead."

MAINTAINING COMMITMENT TO A DISTANT VISION

Carlos's vision provides an interesting contrast to the visions of other teachers discussed in this book. Indeed, his vision may be one of the most distant visions of all those described in this book. Yet, while it is extremely distant, Carlos maintains his commitment, his ideals, and does not lose faith in possibilities. One of the ways Carlos deals with the distance is that he recognizes and appreciates the triumphs and accomplishments he and his students make. He takes pride in their development. Early in his career, he even finds opportunities (as he did in AVID) to gather data that could systematically demonstrate the successes of his students. Yet, at the same time, he is not Pollyanna-ish about the progress he makes. His concern about making sure he does not "sugarcoat" his and his students' gains was evident in his efforts to be sure to present both the areas of strength and those areas needing improvement to the AVID coordinator.

His careful professional decisions in light of his vision also enable him to maintain his commitment and motivation. With his vision in mind, like Jake, he sought out professional opportunities such as the AVID program that he felt would enable him to make progress. He also joined reform-oriented committees at his school to help him (and his school) get closer to his vision.

Like Andrea, Jake, and Kelly, Carlos makes career decisions (like leaving Sandhill High School and moving to Lincoln College Preparatory) that enable him to continue to pursue that vision and to enjoy a sense of momentum and continued accomplishment. Like Jake, Kelly, and Andrea, he uses his vision as a means to evaluate and move to contexts in which he can continue to experience that success. And, like Jake, he does not base his move on a better salary, more manageable workload, or even an opportunity to work with more academically prepared children.

Finally, Carlos's experience reveals a different way in which the tension between students and subject matter can play out in one's vision. Carlos's personal experiences lead to a reframing of the ways in which he envisions helping students learn his subject matter. He sees history as a means to helping Latino students develop the kind of self-confidence and self-awareness he feels is essential to being a strong and successful person. One might argue, though, that his focus upon students might at times overwhelm his focus upon subject—and some might ask whether his students are learning enough history to compete in college once they arrive there. Not everyone would agree with his choice to teach such practical knowledge about schools and colleges over more traditional history or social studies units.

His own experience has clearly led him to some ambivalence about subject matter (although he maintains a passion for history) and, further, to an understanding that subject matter is not the only key to success in school and in life. Carlos would argue that one must understand other things about the educational system in order to succeed. Simply mastering the subject matter is not what his vision is all about, because there is more than that to success in academics and in life.

CHAPTER 6

Taking Vision Into Account

If you don't know where you're going, any path will do.
Anna Richert

Andrea, Carlos, Jake, and Kelly have powerful visions. They imagine students learning about themselves through reading rich literary texts, graduating from high school and making a contribution to their society, having indelible experiences of powerful school learning, and becoming independent and critical thinkers. At times, these visions have helped these teachers uphold extremely high standards for their students and continue to reflect on how to press themselves and their students to learn and grow. Their visions have helped these teachers think about their teaching, maintained their commitment and enthusiasm, and prompted their professional growth. At other times, however, these visions have felt so distant that they have left these teachers riddled with doubt and deeply discouraged.

The good news about these four teachers is that despite their uncertainties and struggles, their visions ultimately helped them learn, imagine what was possible, and sustain them through difficult times. The bad news is that these committed, caring, well-educated, highly qualified teachers (whom many parents would want for their own children) could not easily find places in which they could attain their visions. Many of them were on a continuing search to find places where they could support their students in the kinds of academic work and success they imagined for them. Ultimately, all these teachers left the mainstream public school system. While they have not gone to elite schools in affluent neighborhoods, they have all come to feel that they are unable to attain their visions in traditional public schools.

Yet, despite the role vision plays in teachers' lives, vision is rarely addressed in teacher education programs or in teachers' professional development experiences. Indeed, as Andrea reflected,

> I keep thinking about how this . . . would have been so helpful in my program. Just constantly thinking about this idea of vision . . .

Figure 6.1. Supporting New Teachers Through Vision

When teacher educators give teachers…, teachers can….

Opportunities to surface and explore visions $\longrightarrow$
Probe, examine, and challenge tacit assumptions about teaching

Exposure to new visions $\longrightarrow$ Develop a sense of possibility

Ways to focus upon the gap between vision and practice $\longrightarrow$
Learn strategies to understand and come to terms
with the gap between vision and practice

something to start from. Just imagining where you want to be, but also thinking about where you actually are. And how to look at that discrepancy and see: How far do you have to get from one to the other? What can you do? What's the process in order to achieve your vision?

WHEN TEACHER EDUCATORS TAKE VISION INTO ACCOUNT

There are exceptions, however—teacher educators who support teachers by taking vision into account. In this chapter I will focus on the work of Traci Bliss (Idaho State University), Pamela LePage (San Francisco State University), Rachel Lotan (Stanford University), Jean Lythcott (Stanford University), Anna Richert (Mills College), and Lee Shulman (Stanford University). [1]

When teacher educators (such as the six I profile) give teachers an opportunity to articulate their visions, they enable new teachers to surface and probe their tacit understandings about subject, students, and teaching (see Figure 6.1). When teacher educators share the visions of experienced or innovative teachers, they help new teachers develop a sense of possibility that reaches beyond their own experiences of teaching. And when teacher educators focus upon the gap between vision and practice, they help new teachers understand and come to terms with the gap between vision and practice.

SURFACING AND EXPLORING VISIONS PROVIDE OPPORTUNITIES TO EXAMINE LEARNING

Surfacing visions is particularly important because new teachers already come to teacher preparation with beliefs and assumptions. Many of the teacher educators discussed in this chapter use the concept of vision as a means to understand new teachers' incoming visions—their hopes and dreams. Anna Richert, Rachel Lotan, Traci Bliss, and Pamela LePage all report that they require new students to write about and describe their visions. Jean Lythcott asks her students to draw images of ideal practice. These teacher educators also find that using vision can help new teachers surface and examine their own beliefs.

For instance, at San Francisco State University, Pamela LePage, the codirector of the Mild-Moderate Disabilities master's and teacher credentialing program, asks her student teachers to write and revise a vision statement over the period of their 2-year program. LePage feels that asking her students to articulate their visions provides them with a means to validate and share purposes, and to develop a sense of mutual goals and values (as well as to see the ways in which other student teachers' visions might vary).

It also allows LePage to learn a great deal about her students' thinking about teaching. For instance, upon examining a set of statements from one cohort of 23 of her students, LePage and her research assistant Shelley Nielson found that her students' early vision statements clearly demonstrated commonalities (LePage & Nielson, 2004). Many of the teachers envisioned inclusive schooling for children with special needs and articulated a kind of political commitment to making sure such children had their needs met. Yet at the same time, examining their visions helped LePage see that their visions were somewhat vague and that subject matter was often left out.

In addition, LePage was also able to identify some inconsistencies as well as some beliefs about children with special needs that warranted some exploration and, in some cases, challenge. For example, although many of their vision statements emphasized the goal of inclusion for all students with special needs, their statements suggested that the teachers themselves held conceptions of these children that might make it difficult for them to function in an inclusive classroom. Many of the student teachers viewed disabilities as obstacles to overcome and believed the children felt that way about themselves as well. Furthermore, the student teachers' main goals for their students with special needs were to help the children feel good about themselves, suggesting that the student teachers believed that the children do not feel good about themselves. The teacher candidates were working from the assumption that these children had low esteem and faced insurmountable challenges, and thus their main goals for the students were to transform the students' views of themselves. Surprisingly, LePage's students' visions rarely had to do with children acquiring new knowledge or developing new skills or understandings. In line with that, the student teachers seemed to see their roles in their visions more as helping, empowering, or advocating for students with special needs. In turn, their teaching role received less emphasis.

LePage was concerned that many of these ideas were inconsistent with the teachers' own desires to provide special education students with inclusive education and might contribute to lowered and limited expectations for their students. Surfacing these issues led her to design experiences for her students that would challenge their initial perceptions. She required that they engage in a significant amount of data collection, including interviews with and observations of children with special needs. She required that her students "really talk" to their own students about issues that mattered to them—ask the students questions and then reflect carefully upon what they learned from the students. And she required them to observe their students in a learning environment—all of which she felt was critical in helping her prospective teachers overcome their stereotypical conceptions of children with special needs.

As a result of her carefully designed emphasis upon helping new teachers develop the skills of teacher research (and upon particular experiences such as student interviews), LePage found some changes in the second drafts of their vision statements. Details and depth were emerging, particularly in terms of how they imagined their classroom pedagogy. She also found that her teacher education students' statements were less "certain"—suggesting that perhaps they were more open to questioning their assumptions and to re-examining their perspectives about students with special needs. Finally, she felt that her students were gradually developing more fruitful and beneficial attitudes about students with special needs. For instance, they seemed now to understand that children with special needs had "great strengths" and also that they are in many ways like all children, with interesting personalities, multiple abilities, and different needs.

For Andrea, it was really only later in her career and largely on her own, that she developed such an understanding of her students' interests, abilities, needs, and the circumstances of their lives. Yet if she had encountered teachers like LePage, and had opportunities not only to observe students (as she did have in her education coursework), but also to talk with them, question them, try to understand them, and think about their perspectives, she might have entered the field with a greater understanding of who her students were and what their needs and strengths were. Coupled with opportunities, in turn, to think about the relationship between who those students were and what she wanted to teach, she then might have been able to more successfully plan curriculum that was engaging and appropriate for her particular students at Jefferson. It is an open question what impact such experiences might have had for Andrea and her choices to stay or leave Jefferson. On the other hand, even though the challenge of balancing students and subjects is something that teachers with all levels of experience struggle with throughout their careers, the kind of support LePage's class offered might have provided Andrea with a better foundation for dealing with it.

VISION PROVIDES IMAGES OF THE POSSIBLE

Maxine Greene's quote about a "consciousness of possibility" (1988, p. 23) illustrates the imaginative potential of vision for new teachers: It can raise their expectations and give them a sense of what teachers can do, what they themselves can reach for. A focus upon developing and stretching vision can be particularly important for those teachers who have less fully articulated visions. And, for those teachers who already have a strong sense of vision, being able to further articulate, or even reshape it, may help new teachers think beyond their own apprenticeship of observation in order to stretch their images of practice. Either way, focusing upon vision can provide new teachers a sense of something to reach for in their own future teaching practice.

Lee Shulman, who taught a core foundations course about teaching and learning for over a decade in the Stanford University Teacher Education Program (STEP), used to show his students a videotape made by University of Michigan professor and mathematics teacher Deborah Ball, in which young learners in an elementary classroom are engaged in an extremely sophisticated debate about the concept of even and odd numbers (Ball, 1996). He would pair the viewing of the video with an article, "With an Eye on the Mathematical Horizon: Dilemmas of Teaching Elementary School Mathematics," in which Ball describes the incident and discusses her struggles to balance the needs and readiness of her students with the demands of the subject matter.

Shulman explained that he showed that videotape in part because he wanted students to develop a new set of images of practice that might stand in marked contrast to what they had experienced themselves as students. Afterwards, students often described feeling inspired by Ball's teaching, and mentioned a sense that their imaginations had been stretched after seeing that video. Shulman recalled that his students often remarked that they had a completely new understanding and vision of what good teaching could look like after seeing that video, and he ascribed that visual learning to seeing a real classroom in practice rather than only reading about it (Shulman, 1987).

Shulman also showed Ball's videotape to provide a vision of the possible that, like the early visions of Kelly and Jake, included attention to both students and subject. Indeed, part of what is particularly powerful about Ball's teaching is that she is able to attend closely both to individual student thinking and to the disciplinary concepts with which her students are engaged. Shulman used that videotape as a kind of jumping off point to engage his student teachers in discussions of Bruner's (1960/1977) concept of "intellectual honesty" and the delicate balance between being true to one's subject and recognizing the readiness of one's students. Shulman felt through these discussions, student teachers were developing not only a new sense of the possible, but also a grasp of what it meant to work toward addressing both students and subjects in one's teaching vision.

Both Jake and Kelly reported, after moving to a new school, struggling with the needs and skills of their students and finding an appropriate level of support for their new students, yet still offering deep engagement and a worthy challenge in their subject. They both talked about "relearning" how to approach that balance with their new students. Yet that kind of relearning is harder to prepare new teachers to understand and appreciate. Indeed, one challenge that teacher educators like Shulman and the others included in this chapter often talk about is the difficulty of helping student teachers understand how master teachers like Ball developed that practice. The continuing challenge for teacher educators in such work is how to find ways to enable new teachers to see the steps involved in working toward such practice, and unfortunately, it is difficult to represent that kind of development.

Traci Bliss's Inquiry, Thinking, and Knowing course at Idaho State University illustrates another approach to using vision to challenge new teachers to explore and think beyond their experiences. This foundational philosophy course required for all incoming teacher education students is designed to provide students with some conceptual tools to undergird their classroom visions. One of Traci's first goals, however, is to provide student teachers with examples of practice that might be quite different from those they themselves experienced as students in order to help them consider new alternatives and new visions. She builds the course around videos (Bliss, 2000) of six accomplished National Board Certified teachers, which she and the students view, view again, critique, discuss, and write about throughout the semester. She argues that by helping her student teachers observe (and analyze carefully) real, pedagogically sophisticated classrooms they then are able to imagine new possibilities for themselves, their classroom, their teaching, and their students.

Bliss finds while that her students sometimes struggle with these classrooms that conflict with their incoming visions of good teaching, they are also inspired by such powerful teaching practices. They begin to develop a deeper sense of their own visions and, in some cases, to craft them in new ways. In addition, Bliss feels that having such an inspiring vision of the possible enables new teachers to overcome some of the minor (and major) hurdles because they have a sense of purpose. As she explains, "when you have this clear vision, your sense of the obstacles becomes diminished."[2]

Beyond helping new teachers imagine what is possible, vision can also enable new teachers to develop a sense of direction and purpose for their work. For Bliss, vision serves as a "rudder" for their work:

It's the rudder of the sailboat. Whether it's high wind or low wind, or whatever the external conditions are, the rudder keeps the sailboat on course. What do I go back to? What do I need to hold on to? Without that vision, what ends up happening is that they fall back into the belief that they are technicians . . . . [But with vision] they continue to pursue *the possible*.

Anna Richert of Mills College emphasizes the concept of vision in her course for similar reasons. Vision is an organizing principle for Anna Richert's year-long foundational course required for all students called Introduction to the Profession of Teaching Diverse Students. The first semester is described on the syllabus as "What is your vision?"; the second, "Revisiting your vision"; and the third, "Enacting your vision." Richert believes that asking students to articulate their visions provides them with a basis for the pedagogical decisions and choices they must constantly make: "as I say to my students, 'If you don't know where you're going, it's hard to get there.' " [3] In Dewey's terms, an "end in view" enables one to make thoughtful and purposeful decisions about teaching and learning, and serves as a basis for interactions with individual children.

Richert emphasizes that when a new teacher develops vision, she not only knows where she is going, but she also can develop a sense of when it is appropriate to veer, when it is reasonable to stay put and explore, and when it is important to stay the course and continue to move ahead. She described one student teacher who had been concerned about the time spent in long discussions with her elementary school students. Richert recalled that the student teacher had an "aha!" moment when writing about her vision and the concept of an "end in view." The student teacher realized that she could make decisions about whether or not the discussion they were having was important to pursue or not, in light of the goals and purposes expressed in her vision.

EQUIPPING TEACHERS WITH TOOLS AND STRATEGIES TO DEAL WITH THE GAP

Yet if teachers do not have the tools or strategies to achieve their visions, they may conceive of the gap between vision and practice as too great to overcome. As one new teacher in this study, Sarah, commented, it was extremely discouraging to attend her education courses because she felt that she was not learning the tools and strategies she needed in order to attain the kinds of classrooms she envisioned (and her peers seemed to be able to create): "I would get out of there and I would feel so depressed. I would feel a combination of envy and disappointment in myself." For that reason, teacher educators like Anna Richert, Rachel Lotan, and Jean Lythcott focus upon helping new teachers develop practical and conceptual strategies to begin to bridge the gap.

Richert leads students in preparing to actually enact vision at three levels: that of the teacher, that of the classroom, and that of the school. She invites her students to think about how all these contexts relate, and how vision can—and should—be enacted at all levels of teaching. Richert consistently brings the discussion back to issues of "who are you?" and "what is your vision?" and "what does it mean to live a life that's guided by commitments?"—questions that were certainly at the heart of Carlos's wrenching decision regarding leaving Sandhill High School. At the same time, Richert guides the discussion about vision in terms of creating real classrooms. Her students read articles that weigh the relationship between personal commitments and the classroom. Students discuss the imagined and real classrooms created by those authors in relationship to the one they hope to create. Such conversations can provide some early guidance and support (and perhaps a kind of framework for thinking) for teachers who may later deal with some of the same issues that Carlos faced regarding very tough personal and professional choices around how to accomplish one's vision.

Richert asks them to consider: In what ways can you enact a vision about what it means to teach? They read about and consider different classroom instantiations of visions. They talk about schools, reading (among other pieces) excerpts from Deborah Meier's book *The Power of Their Ideas* (2000). With that piece as a reference point, student teachers discuss their own responsibility to engage in school conversations about how things ought to be. They consider how their own school could be shaped to help them enact their visions. Richert also brings to bear upon the discussion McLaughlin and Talbert's (1993) concept of "nested contexts" so that student teachers begin to understand the challenges that teachers like Kelly faced that are inherent in implementing a vision in a classroom that is impacted by the school culture, the community, the state, and the nation.

Some teacher educators find that helping new teachers examine their visions in light of professional and state standards can be particularly useful in helping them think about how they will teach. For example, some courses engage student teachers in an assignment called "domain mapping" (Shepard et al., 2005). Starting with the state's curriculum frameworks or national content standards, teachers draw a Venn diagram or construct a table to illustrate what section of their desired curriculum is covered by the test and what is not. This activity helps them understand what parts of their curriculum are—and are not—represented by state or commercially developed tests. Student teachers can then see, for example, that if a test may cover the easiest-to-measure part of their subject, this does not mean that every aspect of the subject has been adequately represented. Examining what has been left out helps to make clear the relationship between their own goals and purposes, as expressed in their vision, and the demands of the required tests as well as the limitations of the test as a curriculum guide. Based on this explicit analysis, student teachers can then consciously plan curriculum (as well as allocate their teaching time) in ways that not only attend to tested content but that keep it in its proportional place. An activity like this is particularly useful in that it prepares student teachers to do the kind of careful examinations of state tests that Kelly found so useful in balancing her own curriculum with state requirements.

Andrea, Carlos, Kelly, and Jake's experiences also suggest another way that teacher educators might draw upon vision to help support new teachers. These teachers' visions were a key tool in helping them analyze and identify school sites in which they would most likely feel at home and feel successful. Not all teachers have a choice of where to teach. But if teacher educators can help new teachers articulate their visions and consider what an appropriate match might be, and help new teachers analyze the visions of the school sites and their potential colleagues, those teachers might have a greater likelihood of ending up in places where they could more successfully navigate the demands, challenges, and emotions of their chosen profession.

This is not to suggest that it is not appropriate or healthy to teach in contexts that prompt interrogations of visions and even challenge them. Such experiences may be particularly powerful for student teachers, given that they are provided ample opportunity for reflection and thoughtfully supported in their efforts and inquiries. Yet it seems clear that substantial conflicts (such as those experienced by Andrea) can result in drastic consequences not only for a teacher's dreams and for her career as a teacher, but also for her learning and that of her students.

At the Stanford University Teacher Education Program, program director Rachel Lotan and science educator Jean Lythcott contend that enabling student teachers to think about their visions in light of their student teaching sites enables them to begin to articulate—and thus better understand—the nature of the gap between vision and reality. Lotan and Lythcott feel that the public, communal experience of discussing those gaps with their fellow students is particularly critical. They note that student teachers can better come to terms with some of their disappointments as well as the pleasant surprises in terms of what they feel they might accomplish. The students learn that they are not the only ones struggling with the gap, and they begin to share strategies with one another. Lotan and Lythcott also feel that students can begin to get an understanding not only of the reasons they come to teaching and the ideals that may shape their beginning practice, but also of the areas where they might need work and support in further developing visions.

DEVELOPING INDIVIDUAL VISION IN LIGHT
OF PROGRAM VISION

The work of these teacher educators also suggests a lesson for program design in teacher education. These six teacher educators who help new teachers develop personal visions have all also worked hard with their colleagues to develop a program vision in order to guide their work. They argue that teacher educators themselves need to have a sense of the kind of teaching they hope to support in their program, and the kind of visions of teaching they hope their students will develop. Indeed, recent research on a small set of exceptional teacher education programs suggests that one common element of such programs was the existence of a common vision of good teaching (Darling-Hammond, 2000).

As the director of a program faculty that has recently made significant efforts to develop and articulate a shared program vision, Rachel Lotan points out that having such a program vision does not mean that all student teachers must then "accept," learn, and parrot back the program's vision unquestionably. Rather, it means having a sense of the kinds of powerful approaches, ideas, and practices of teaching and learning that a teacher education faculty would want new teachers to encounter, consider, and experience as part of developing their own personal visions. Lotan distinguishes between programs that have a *vision* and those that have an *ideology*—explaining that the former is one that welcomes debate, argumentation, and probing of differences, rather than blind acceptance and the smoothing over of disagreement and conflict. She argues that differences and conflicts can promote powerful learning, and can ultimately enable new teachers to develop more informed, robust, and thoughtful personal visions of teaching.

Indeed, such experiences in navigating the differences between program vision and personal vision may provide some grounding for new teachers who will eventually face similar future situations. They will often encounter times in which they need to balance the needs and requirements of their own vision with the visions held by others. As Anna Richert explains, if her new teachers have a sense of vision, they will be able to have a strong and compelling voice in educational debates in which other visions and voices will certainly be at play.

Focusing upon teachers' vision may help us to discern why committed, thoughtful teachers consider leaving the profession, as well as why equally committed and thoughtful teachers remain inspired in their work. But perhaps even more important, teachers' vision may also provide us with a particularly powerful means of focusing upon the support and sustenance of new teachers, by enabling us to validate their commitments, challenge and deepen their beliefs about teaching and learning, and imagine the steps they need to take to move closer to their ideals.

Methodology:
How Can We Hear
What Other People See?

In our everyday experience, visions held by political or religious leaders are highly public and accessible—shared in public speeches, on television, in newspapers, or even sometimes in advertisements. But teachers' visions are usually quite the opposite. The private quality of teachers' vision posed a number of challenges for this research. How could I examine a set of images that, far from being readily apparent in practice, were both personally intimate and publicly invisible? Furthermore, the very notion of vision suggested that it was quite distant from everyday work. How could I as a researcher uncover those ideas and images?

TALKING ABOUT VISION

The question "How can we hear what other people see?" represents the first methodological issue I had to address: the appropriateness of language as a medium for exploring and communicating teachers' visions. Scholars of visual communication suggest that language—rather than images—may in some cases serve as a more appropriate means for hearing what people see. For example, Messaris (1994) argues that language has some important advantages over images, particularly in conveying complex ideas. While pictures are better suited to convey specific instances, he argues, language is often more appropriate for conveying generalizations and abstractions. Language can provide important contextual information, as well as convey negative instances or absences. Finally, language can convey nonvisual experiences as well, such as emotions, tactile sensations, or auditory experiences.

On the other hand, some of my colleagues have found that asking teachers to draw or illustrate their images of teaching was successful (Lythcott, 2004; Whyte & Ellis, 2004). Although sometimes participants worry that their artistic skills are not good enough, these teacher educators found that the activity often enables teachers to communicate some aspects of their vision that are easier to express in symbols and images than in words. Perhaps in future work, a combination of writing and drawing tasks might be best used to capture visions.

WHOSE VISIONS TO HEAR?

In selecting the participants for this study, I deliberately selected a group of teachers whose visions seemed to be most clearly articulated and vivid. I felt that investigating relatively articulated visions might enable me to learn more about the characteristics, role, and sources of vision than exploring the vision of a participant who described a vision which was not as rich or well-defined. I also sought to select participants who represented a range of levels of experience, subject matter expertise, and teacher education programs.

The survey participants were 80 student teachers and alumni from two teacher education programs: one, a private university masters' degree program; and the other, a state university credentialling program. Selecting teachers from two different teacher education programs was important in order for my participants to be representative of a variety of educational experiences. The student teachers were all students who attended the mandatory foundations courses required by each of the two teacher education programs. The novice and veteran teachers were all teachers who responded to the survey mailed to them. I chose to work with teachers at several points in their careers: student teachers, novice teachers, and veteran teachers. Examining teachers early and later in their careers allowed me to explore a range of visions from those that might have been crystalizing to those that were more deeply evolved. And in order to vary participants along other contexts, I selected my "portrait case" participants to reflect different subject matters: English (Andrea), history (Jake and Carlos), mathematics (Carlos), and science (Kelly).

HOW CAN I HEAR WHAT OTHER PEOPLE ENVISION?

I collected data from five sources to help me hear what my participants envisioned. The data for the 16 brief case participants came from the written descriptions of their visions from the survey (see Appendix B) and an initial and a follow-up interview. The interviews were designed to take place over time to capture any changes or developments in vision: The first interviews

Table A.1. Sources of Data

Data Type	Survey Teachers	Brief Case Teachers	Portrait Teachers
Vision statement (spring 1997)	√	√	√
Initial interview (summer 1997)		√	√
Follow-up interview (winter 1998)		√	√
Classroom observations (spring 1998)			√
Reflective interviews (spring 1998)			√
Feedback interviews (spring 1999, summer 2005)			√
Yearly check-in interviews (summers of 1999, 2000–2005)			√

with the 16 brief case teachers were conducted in summer 1997 with follow-up interviews in winter 1998.

With the portrait participants, I also collected data from classroom observations and participants' reflections before and after the visits (see Table A.1). These multiple sources provided me with a number of windows into the teachers' visions and a number of occasions on which to check the reliability of the picture of their visions that was emerging. Classroom observations and additional interviews with the four portrait case teachers were conducted in spring 1998.

Then I conducted feedback interviews with the four portrait case teachers in spring 1999 to give them an opportunity to correct any factual errors about their visions in my early writing for this study. Equally important, those interviews enabled me to check with them as to whether my analysis of their experience was accurate: Did it ring true? Did it reasonate with them? I conducted a second set of feedback interviews in summer 2005 so that the teachers could provide feedback on the chapters in this book.

I continued to interview the portrait case teachers yearly each summer for 7 years, from 1999 through 2005, in order to learn about any changes or developments in their visions as well as to investigate the continued role vision played in their lives in their career decisions and their teaching.

Vision Statement Writing Prompt

I developed the following set of prompts for this research in order to help teachers describe their visions. All 80 teachers in the initial part of this study responded to these questions, as did the 4 teachers portrayed in depth in this book. When I used it with the teachers, each question was placed at the top of a new sheet of paper to give teachers ample room to respond to each question.

> These questions are designed to elicit your images of the ideal classroom. Please feel free to describe in the next few pages what you dream about or hope for even though it may be somewhat—or even very—different from your current classroom. I'd like you to begin by envisioning this ideal classroom for a moment. Suppose, akin to a "virtual reality tour," you can imagine yourself walking into your classroom. You can look around the room, and you can hear and see the activities going on . . .

What do you see, feel, and hear when you walk around your ideal classroom?

What are you doing in your ideal classroom? What is your role? Why?

What are your students doing in this ideal classroom? What role(s) do the students play? Why?

What kinds of things are the students learning in your ideal classroom? For instance, what topics or texts are they working on? Why are those important for them to learn?

What is the relationship between what goes on in your ideal classroom and the kind of society you would like to see in the twenty-first century?

Notes

Chapter 2

1. Jefferson High School, which is a large comprehensive high school in northern California, serves a low-income population of students. The largest number of students at the school are African American (30%) followed by White (27%) and Hispanic (26%), and a small population of Asian students (8%).

2. Indeed, Andrea has remained at St. Mark's and has now been teaching English for 7 years as of the printing date of this book.

Chapter 3

1. This was before California pursued the Public Schools Accountability Act (April 1999), which involves similar testing of students through tests such as the SAT-9, and ranking schools along an Academic Performance Index (API). For more information, see the California Department of Education's website about the act: http://www.edsource.org/pub_edf_psaa.cfm.

2. The MCAS science test for 1998 required students to be familiar with "Inquiry" along with three "Domains of Science" (Physical Sciences, Life Sciences, Earth and Space Sciences), Technology, and "Science, Technology, and Human Affairs." (For more information and for specific test items see the Massachusetts Department of Education website about the 1998 MCAS test: http://www.doe.mass.edu/mcas/1998/release/1.pdf.)

3. Students' scores on the MCAS are reported in terms of percentages of students determined to be Advanced, Proficient, Needs Improvement, and Failing. In 1998, of the 56 Hilltop students who took the science exam, 77% were scored as Failing and 23% were scored as Needs Improvement; none were scored as either Proficient or Advanced. In 1999, of the 50 Hilltop students who took the science exam, 83% were scored as Failing, 17% as Needs Improvement, and none as Proficient or Advanced. The results did not improve in 2000. Although a few more students took the exam (57) than the previous year, 86% were scored as Failing, 14% as Needs Improvement, and none as Proficient or Advanced. These very low scores were fairly consistent across subject areas—in 1998, for example, 56 students took the math exams and 98% were scored as Failing, 2% as Needs Improvement, and none as Proficient or Advanced. While 11% of the 56 who took the English exams were scored as Proficient, still 68%

were scored as Failing and 21% as Needs Improvement (Massachusetts Department of Education, 2000a). In addition, the Hilltop science scores were quite similar to the science scores for the entire district of Boston in 2000; none of the district's students scored at the Advanced level, 11% qualified as Proficient, 24% as Needs Improvement, and 54% as Failing (Massachusetts Department of Education, 2000b).

4. The state has not published the science scores for the years 2001 and after, so unfortunately it is not possible to determine how Kelly's students did on these tests as she continued to work with them.

Chapter 4

1. The Coalition of Essential Schools (CES) is a reform organization founded by Theodore Sizer with the goal of reforming public education, particularly at the high school level. Schools that join the Coalition agree to work toward the "Common Principles," a series of principles that undergird CES reform: personalize instruction; develop small schools and classrooms; evaluate student learning through multiple authentic assessments; and support learning through the completion of common and authentic tasks. (See http://www.essentialschools.org for more information on the Coalition of Essential Schools.)

Chapter 5

1. Although Carlos was prepared and certified to teach social studies (9–12) and was hired to teach social studies, he was also invited to run a summer program in mathematics. Asking teachers to teach "out-of-field," while common to some degree in all schools, is a practice more often found in urban districts serving students of color and lower income (Lankford et al., 2002; National Commission on Teaching and America's Future, 1996). Therefore, while he believed that his vision encompassed all parts of his teaching (including mathematics), his passion and his strong subject matter knowledge was in history.

2. This is a reference to California's Proposition 227, which had passed just the night before, requiring that all public school instruction be conducted only in English.

3. AVID is an "in-school support system for grades 5–12 that prepares students for college eligibility and success. AVID places academically average students in advanced classes. AVID levels the playing field for minority, rural, low-income and other students without a college-going tradition in their families. AVID is for all students, but it targets those in the academic middle. AVID is implemented schoolwide and districtwide." For more information, see the AVID website: http://www.avidonline.org/info/?tabid=1&ID=548 (retrieved October 21, 2003).

4. Lincoln College Preparatory's mission focuses explicitly upon preparing underachieving students for college success.

Chapter 6

1. Several of these examples are based upon papers presented in a symposium on vision that I chaired called "The Underexplored Role of Vision in Learning to Teach: Teacher Educators Taking Vision into Account" in April 2004 in San Diego at the American Educational Research Association annual meeting. Additional examples are drawn from interviews conducted in 2003 with two of these teacher educators.

2. Quotes from Traci Bliss are from the transcript of an interview I conducted with her about her teacher education course on April 11, 2003, in Menlo Park, California, at the Carnegie Foundation for the Advancement of Teaching.

3. Quotes from Anna Richert are from the transcript of an interview I conducted with her about her teacher education course on July 24, 2003, in Menlo Park, California, at the Carnegie Foundation for the Advancement of Teaching.

References

Abrams, L. M., Pedulla, J. J., & Madaus, G. F. (2003). Views from the classroom: Teachers' opinions of statewide testing programs. *Theory Into Practice, 42*(1), 18–29.

Austin, K. (1997). *Experimentation in practice: A cross-case analysis of veteran teachers' experiences with Fostering a Community of Learners.* Stanford, CA: Stanford University and WestEd.

Ball, D. (1993). With an eye on the mathematical horizon: Dilemmas of teaching elementary school mathematics. *Elementary School Journal, 93*(4), 373–397.

Ball, D. (1996). Sean Numbers multimedia package [VHS & print materials]. Ann Arbor, MI: Mathematics Teaching and Learning to Teach Project, University of Michigan.

Bliss, T. (2000). *Idaho Classrooms of Accomplished Teachers* (6 videotapes). Pocatello, ID: Classrooms of Accomplished Teachers Project, Idaho State University. [Available from Insight Communications Company, 810 Seventh Avenue, 71st Floor, New York, NY 10019]

Britzman, D. (1991). *Practice makes practice.* Albany: State University of New York Press.

Bruner, J. (1960/1977). *The process of education.* Cambridge, MA: Harvard University Press.

Coburn, C. (2001). Collective sensemaking about reading: How teachers mediate reading policy in their professional communities. *Educational Evaluation and Policy Analysis, 23*(2), 145–170.

Damasio, A. R. (1994). *Descartes' error.* New York: Putnam.

Darling-Hammond, L. (Ed.) (2000). *Studies of excellence in teacher education* (Vols. 1–3). Washington, DC: American Association of Colleges for Teacher Education.

Duffy, G. (1998). Teaching and the balancing of round stones. *Phi Delta Kappan 79*(10), 777–780.

Evans, R. (1996). *The human side of school change.* San Francisco: Jossey-Bass.

Fullan, M. (1993). *Change forces.* London: Falmer Press.

Greene, M. (1988). *Dialectic of freedom.* New York: Teachers College Press.

Grissmer, D., & Kirby, S. (1997). Teacher turnover and teacher quality. *Teachers College Record, 99*, 45–56.

Hammerness, K. (1997). *When visions collide: The struggle to see theory in practice.* Report on "Fostering a Community of Learners" Project (Vol. 3, No. 5). Stanford, CA: Stanford University and WestEd.

Hargreaves, A. (1994). *Changing teachers, changing times: Teachers' work and culture in the postmodern age*. New York: Teachers College Press.

Hargreaves, A. (1998). The emotions of teaching and educational change. In A. Hargreaves et al. (Eds.), *International handbook of educational change* (Vol. 1, pp. 558–575). Dordrecht, the Netherlands: Kluwer Academic Publishers.

Haycock, K. (2000). No more settling for less. *Thinking 6–16, 4*(1), 3–12.

Huberman, M. (1993). *The lives of teachers* (J. Neufeld, Trans.). New York: Teachers College Press.

Ingersoll, R. M. (2001). Teacher turnover and teacher shortages: An organizational analysis. *American Educational Research Journal, 38*(3), 499–534.

Johnson, S. M., & Birkeland, S. E. (2002, April). *Pursuing a "Sense of Success": New teachers explain their career decisions.* Paper presented at the annual meeting of the American Educational Research Association, New Orleans, LA.

Jones, G., Jones, B., Hardin, B., Chapman, L., Yarborough, T., & Davis, M. (1999). The impact of high-stakes testing on teachers and students in North Carolina. *Phi Delta Kappan, 81*(3), 199–203.

Koretz, D., Barron, S., Mitchell, K., & Steecher, B. (1996). *The perceived effects of the Kentucky Instructional Results Information System (KIRIS)* (MR-792–PCT/FF). Santa Monica, CA: RAND.

Lankford, H., Loeb, S., & Wyckoff, J. (2002). Teacher sorting and the plight of urban schools: A descriptive analysis. *Educational Evaluation and Policy Analysis, 24*(1), 37–62.

LePage, P., & Nielson, S. (2004, April). *The development of vision in special education.* Paper presented at the annual meeting of the American Educational Research Assocation, San Diego, CA.

Little, J. W. (1996). The emotional contours and career trajectories of (disappointed) reform enthusiasts. *Cambridge Journal of Education, 26*(3), 345–359.

Lortie, D. (1975). *Schoolteacher: A sociological study.* Chicago: University of Chicago Press.

Louis, K. S., & Miles, M. B. (1990). *Improving the urban school: What works and why.* New York: Teachers College Press.

Lythcott, J. (2004, April). *Becoming a teacher: A new scrutiny.* Paper presented at the annual meeting of the American Educational Research Association, San Diego, CA.

Massachusetts Department of Education. (2000a, November). Spring 2000 MCAS tests: Report of 1998–2000 school results. Retrieved September 4, 2002, from http://www.doe.mass.edu/mcas/2000/results/9800sd/sc10_9800.pdf

Massachusetts Department of Education (2000b, November). Summary of district performance. Retrieved July 11, 2005, from http://www.doe.mass.edu/mcas/2000/results/dperf00.pdf

McLaughlin, M. W., & Talbert, J. E. (1993). *Contexts that matter for teaching and learning.* Stanford, CA: Stanford University, Center for Research on the Context of Secondary School Teaching.

McMillan, J. H., Myran, S., & Workman, D. (1999). *The impact of mandated statewide testing on teachers' classroom assessment and instructional practices.* Paper presented at the annual meeting of the American Educational Research Association, Montreal, Canada.

Meier, D. (2002). *The power of their ideas: Lessons for America from a small school in Harlem.* Boston, MA: Beacon Press.

Messaris, P. (1994). *Visual "literacy": Image, mind, and reality.* Boulder, CO: Westview Press.

Moffett, K. (1999). *Learning to make waves while learning to swim: New teachers in reforming The light and dark side of a novice teacher learning community.* Paper presented at the annual meeting of the American Educational Research Association, San Diego, CA.

Moffett, K., & Hammerness, K. (1998). *Inspiring emotions and disquieting passions: The light and dark side of a novice teacher learning community.* Paper presented at the annual meeting of the American Educational Research Association, San Diego, CA.

National Commission on Teaching and America's Future. (1996). *What matters most: Teaching for America's future.* New York: Author.

Sacks, O. (1995). *An anthropologist on Mars.* Toronto: Alfred A. Knopf.

Senge, P. (1990). *The fifth discipline.* New York: Doubleday.

Shepard, L., Hammerness, K., Darling-Hammond, L., Rust, F., with Baratz-Snowden, J., Gordon, E., Guttierez, C., & Pacheco, A. (2005). Assessment. In L. Darling-Hammond, J. Bransford, P. LePage, K. Hammerness, & H. Duffy (Eds.), *Preparing teachers for a changing world* (pp. 275–326). San Francisco: Jossey-Bass.

Shulman, L. S. (1986). Those who understand: Knowledge growth in teaching. *Educational Researcher, 17*(1), 4–14.

Shulman, L. S. (1987). Knowledge and teaching: Foundations of the new reform. *Harvard Educational Review, 57*(1), 1–22.

Spillane, J. P., Reiser, B. J., & Reimer, T. (2002). Policy implementation and cognition: Reframing and refocusing implementation research. *Review of Educational Research, 72*(3), 387–431.

Veenman, S. (1984). Perceived problems of beginning teachers. *Review of Educational Research, 54*(2), 143–178.

Wilson, S., Shulman, L., & Richert, A. (1987). "150 Different ways" of knowing: Representations of knowledge in teaching. In J. Calderhead (Ed.), *Exploring teachers' thinking* (pp. 104–124). Eastborne, England: Cassell.

Whyte, A., & Ellis, N. (2004, April). *Representing the teaching of writing.* Paper presented at the annual meeting of the American Educational Research Association, San Diego, CA.

Index

About the Author

Karen Hammerness is a postdoctoral fellow at Stanford University. Her research focuses upon teacher education practice and policy, as well as the relationship between teachers' ideals, their practice, and their careers. She has published a number of journal articles on teachers' visions as well as on the pedagogy of teacher education. In addition, she has coauthored several chapters in *Teaching for Understanding: Linking Research with Practice* (1998), edited by Martha Stone Wiske, and *Preparing Teachers for a Changing World: What Teachers Should Know and Be Able to Do* (2005), which she also coedited with Linda Darling-Hammond, John Bransford, and others. She lives in Westchester County, New York, with her husband and three daughters.